DID I GET OUT OF BED FOR THIS?

DID I GET OUT OF BED FOR THIS?

DAVID EDWARDS

NE✗GEN®

Building the New Generation of Believers

COOK COMMUNICATIONS MINISTRIES
Colorado Springs, Colorado • Paris, Ontario
KINGSWAY COMMUNICATIONS LTD
Eastbourne, England

NexGen® is an imprint of
Cook Communications Ministries, Colorado Springs, CO 80918
Cook Communications, Paris, Ontario
Kingsway Communications, Eastbourne, England

DID I GET OUT OF BED FOR THIS?
© 2004 by David Edwards

First Printing, 2004
Printed in the United States of America
1 2 3 4 5 6 7 8 9 10 Printing/Year 08 07 06 05 04

Unless otherwise noted Scripture quotations are taken from the NEW
AMERICAN STANDARD BIBLE®, Copyright © 1960, 1962, 1963,
1968, 1971, 1972, 1973, 1975, 1977, 1995 by The Lockman
Foundation. Used by permission. Scripture quotations marked KJV are
taken from *King James Version*, Public Domain;

Cataloging-in-Publication Data on file with the Library of Congress

ISBN 0781441390

*To **Flipopoly:** You've lived life with a godly passion and confidence that has enabled me to see the answers to life that never fail. I'm forever grateful.*

*To **Richard and Marilyn:** The heart holds the most important commitments in life. The friendship we share rises to the top of my heart. Thanks for being my committed friends and for helping me know how to answer the questions for life.*

Contents

CONTENTS

ACKNOWLEDGMENTS

I couldn't have written this book alone. Here are some of the people who helped make it happen.

Trey Bowden: Well, I guess I won't miss a chance to say thank you for your friendship and the great partnership in ministry. Most of all, for watering the rocks in my head.

Janet Lee: You had the vision and insight to set this project in motion. You believed in the value of these books and the impact they will have on thousands of people seeking answers to the questions of life.

Trevor Bron: You took my loaves and fishes and helped multiply them beyond my wildest dreams. A single book becomes a series. Thanks for blessing my life.

Bobby McGraw: I'm still struggling to find your breaking point. Full-time student, pastor—and you still had the time and energy to transcribe this entire project. Wouldn't have happened without you. Your work has been stellar.

Jim Lynch Everybody! You're my friend, my personal doctor who kept me alive—and you drove the comedy engine so well. Better peace through science. Thanks to Eric and Jim Hawkins, for the extra comedy fuel; it helped keep the engine going.

Gary Wilde: Thank you for your surgical editing skills. You preserved the integrity of the manuscripts, communicating the truths that needed to be told, while laughing at my jokes.

Shawn Mathenia: You finally got your very own line in one of my books. *This is it.* Thank you for your friendship and for looking out for me.

Ken Baugh and Frontline: Thank you for your continued passion that shows up in your ongoing work to reach a new generation. You guys are my home away from no home.

The Sound Tracks: Train, Dave Matthews Band, Dave Koz, The Rippingtons, and Journey. Thanks for the inspiration.

The Questions for Life Series

I had just finished speaking at the White House and was eating lunch at Union Station with a young political consultant. We were halfway through our meal when I asked her, "What's life like for a postmodern inside the Beltway? You know, what kinds of questions do they ask?"

"They ask questions about the suffering and wrong in the world," she said, "about the church, and about who Jesus really is. You know, the questions that never fade."

Questions that never fade

Her label for those questions rose up inside of me, and this series of books flowed from that conversation. Postmoderns come wired with the need to answer the questions you'll find in these pages.

Most postmoderns have rejected the pat answers offered by today's spiritual leaders because they have found them to be inadequate for the daily life they face. They have seen others who accepted the ready-made answers but who still struggle making life work. They have no desire to repeat such mistakes. Instead, they challenge the real-life validity of the quick and easy answers.

The questions remain, but some of the questioners let their need for adequate answers diminish into the background. They give way to an apathy that says, "I've got more important things to do in my life than pursuing life's big questions." For others, finding resolution remains a priority. Yet even for them, life can become a never-ending "round-robin" of seeking solutions through new experiences.

Regardless of where you are at the moment, realize that the questions for life never truly fade away. They keep coming back, especially amidst your most trying times. They will keep knocking at your heart's door until you turn and acknowledge their crucial role in finding the life of your dreams. Until you take hold of real explanations, you'll remain constantly searching for the answers that never fail.

Answers that never fail

Spoken or unspoken, identified or unidentified, real answers are priceless. Until we find them, we're haunted by a lack of resolution in life. This unsettled life suffers constant turmoil and never-ending trouble. We look for direction that seems nonexistent, and this makes many of our decisions hard to live with. What price would we pay for a better way?

It's possible to spend a lifetime searching and never finding. Therefore, some would say that the reward comes not in the security of reaching the goal, but in the striving to obtain it. To these people I say: Why waste your life *looking* when you could be *living?*

The Creator of the universe holds the indelible answers we seek. They are not hidden, but they have often been obscured. They are veiled by some who place a higher value on *knowing* the answers than upon allowing the answers to change their lives. We need to push through and ask: What is the actual value of discovering answers that never fail? We'll find the value shining through in *what the answers produce in our lives.* When we discover these answers, our lives change in four supernatural ways. Finding them ...

Builds our outlook It's impossible to live a satisfying life without faith, meaning, and purpose. That's why each of us will place our faith in something or someone that is our primary value. We believe this person or thing will bring meaning and purpose to our life.

Without purpose, we'd have no reason to exist. So even the most cynical and withdrawn person seeks meaning in life. It may reside in something as mundane as keeping a pet iguana fat and happy. Or it could be that he finds meaning in something as twisted as making records and sleeping with young boys.

But life without an ultimate meaning and purpose becomes fragmented and chaotic. We roam from place to place, relationship to relationship, experience to experience, hoping to find something worth living for that endures. The iguana won't live forever. We also quickly discover that people fail us, that work is never-ending, that merely accumulating sensory experiences leads us down a continually darkening pathway.

There is no sense to life without meaning and purpose. There is no meaning and purpose without faith. And there is no faith until we answer the questions that never fade.

Brings ownership Discovering answers to the questions for life transforms us from merely being alive to actually having a life to live. We've all seen people who seem to just take up space in the world. They live for no apparent purpose. The things they do carry no meaning and make no appreciable impact on the people around them. They are alive, but they do not own a life.

> "Ownership of life begins when our head and our heart come together at a long-sought crossroads: where the questions that never fade meet the answers that never fail."

The questions for life can't be glibly answered, nor should they be made impotent through intellect. They must be answered in our hearts; they must settle down into the very center of our person. Ownership of life begins when our head and our heart come together at a long-sought crossroads: where the questions that never fade meet the answers that never fail.

Breaks us open Every question for life has a spiritual dimension. We may assume that answering the question of world hunger and suffering is only a physical matter, but that would be a wrong assumption. This question first finds its answer in a spiritual dimension, then the physical needs can be addressed in practical action. The same is true for all other questions for life; they each have a spiritual dimension.

The questions for life demand *powerful* answers that remain *present,* regardless of circumstance. The answers that never fade literally open us up to the things of God. That is, they lead us to find and apply his *power* and *presence* to the very heart of our question. These answers don't create despair; they settle disputes. They don't cause confusion; they construct a viable contract between life and us.

Brings an outworking Answering the questions for life develops an internal faith expressed in our observable behaviors. In other words, when we own the answers that never fail, our life takes on a meaning that others see and desire. This outworking of faith is extremely practical. It influences the choices we make, the words we speak, and the attitudes we reflect in daily life.

And this outworking can't help but grow a deep confidence within us. When never-failing solutions calm our internal struggles, we are able to move forward amidst seemingly insurmountable odds. We can work in an environment hostile to the things of Christ—and still live out our faith. We are confident that, although those around us may reject us, we are forever accepted by the One who matters most.

In these books, I have refused to "reheat" the old teachings. Instead of serving leftovers, I've dished up biblical answers that really do apply to the lives we live. These books keep it real, and I've written them with you in mind. I've used generous doses of humor and plenty of anecdotes (most of which actually happened to me).

I've made scant reference to other Christian authors, though, for a reason. In my attempt to make these books fresh, I chose to keep them uncluttered by the thoughts of others. Instead, I try to communicate God's thoughts from the Bible straight to your heart.

You'll notice that the title of each book forms a question. The titles of each chapter also appear as questions. But the content of each chapter *answers* that chapter's question. When read in their entirety, the chapters together answer the big question posed by each book.

You can read these books in any order; they each stand on their own in dealing with a single topic. At the end of each book you'll find questions that I hope will encourage an expanded discussion of the subject matter. Why not bring a group of friends together to talk things through?

Although this book series began over lunch inside the Beltway of Washington, D.C., I am aware that we are all bound together by the questions that never fade. As you read, I hope you will find the answers that never fail.

David Edwards
Summer, 2004

INTRODUCTION TO
DID I GET OUT OF BED FOR THIS?

I'm a member of both the local and global church. I have the life I do because the church has given it to me. The culture of the church has shaped me along with all the traveling and speaking I've done for the past twelve years. I've done it through the church, for the expansion of the church, and by the authority, backing, and support of the church. The best things that ever happened to me resulted from my church involvement.

At the same time, the worst wounds I've ever suffered came at the hands of "godly" church people. So I'm not shocked that our generation is leaving the church. I am not stunned when I hear their stories of extreme church people who claim to love God but act so unloving. Nor am I surprised to hear so often: "I'm *never* going back."

If we trace church history accurately, we'll realize we own part of the blame for this mass exodus. The period of the Crusades made the church look strangely similar to the Tony Soprano family, as it strong-armed people into submission. Inquisitions followed the Crusades and produced even higher drama as hapless citizens faced doctrinal litmus tests on a life-or-death grading scale.

In our more recent history, we've watched television-preacher scandals and tolerated sexual abuse among church leaders. We've seen priests accused of immorality moved around as if they're in the witness protection program. The Episcopal Church recently elected the first openly gay bishop. In addition to the denomination-wide rift this election caused, there is now a church-wide ban on playing chess, since Episcopals can't seem to tell the difference between a bishop and a queen. I've got to tell you, I'm not shocked.

This book is not a defense of the things that have happened in church history. And it's certainly not my attempt to explain all of the decisions of the church. Instead, I intend to address the most relevant questions to the church today.

This book springs from two encounters I had in different parts of America. The first occurred earlier this year when I was talking with a young adult who told me his experience of going to church. He said:

> I got up one morning and went to a church that I had heard was really great. I sat there and it just seemed like the whole service was on auto-pilot. People got up, sang some songs, and the music sounded great. Then the guy got up and gave us some helpful advice. He told us how to be better people, and I sat there waiting for something to happen. Nothing happened. The service was over, and everyone got up and left. I thought to myself, *Did I get out of bed for this?*

A friend of mine on the West Coast formed a spiritual friendship with someone in her apartment complex. The man was a professional athlete, as well as a professional real-estate developer, and had done quite well for himself. Over time, through the normal interactions of this friendship, the subject of Jesus had come up. My friend explained how Christ enters into our lives and changes us from the inside out. She bought her friend a Bible and asked him to read through it, using the margin notes to understand it better. She told him simply to listen for the heart of God in what he read. Then she left for a couple weeks of vacation.

When she came back to town, she invited her friend to her church, a church that had a formal feel to it, with lots of tradition and pomp and circumstance. They walked down a long aisle and approached a pew with some open seating. A lady was sitting next to the open seats, and the man asked, "Are these seats saved?"

The lady replied, "I don't know; we'll have to ask."

The man was stunned and didn't know what to say. They eventually found a place to sit as the service began. He did his

> **The pastor got up and told some stories about his family and shared some good suggestions about how to live.**

best to join in singing some hymns. Then the pastor got up and told some stories about his family and shared some good suggestions about how to live. The offering plates came by, and they dropped some money in. They listened to a few announcements before the organ played and everyone left.

After it was over, the guy turned to my friend and said, "I was really hoping that we could read the Bible today." Not once during the entire service had a Bible been opened! Behind his comment was the question, "Did I get out of bed for this?"

The driving question behind both of my encounters is the very real question about why we should even bother with church. It is our responsibility as Christ-followers to redefine the role our church ought to play in our current society. Are we really supposed to show video clips, expect people to scrape together a useful application, and somehow learn to be better people? (I have to tell you, I really don't see how the scene in "Driven," where Sylvester Stallone laps the track picking up quarters with his tires, can help me find change in my car for a tollbooth.) Does the church simply become another reality show for people to watch? Isn't there a higher purpose for an effective Single's Ministry than imitating "Average Joe"? Are we producing TV shows or people? Should we simply be content that at least the church still has some entertainment value like the Super Bowl, presidential elections, and embedded reporters on live military maneuvers?

> **"Does the church simply become another reality show for people to watch? ... Are we producing TV shows or people?"**

On the whole, it seems the church has bought into the idea that bigger is better, that more is merrier, that glitzy means better quality, and that loudness somehow increases the comprehension of those in attendance. We now focus on commercial marketing techniques to create giant object lessons, hoping to prove that the church is still alive and well on planet earth. I've seen people execute fundraisers in church that would make a politician blush.

Recently I read about a church that employed a high-wire act to put on their show. They set up in the parking lot and swung back and forth, high over the pavement. They did all this to drive home the point that "life is filled with ups and downs, but God is the net below you." I also ran across a story of a pastor who wanted to illustrate his point that Satan's temptations are powerless unless we act on them. How did he do it? By holding a gun (loaded with blanks) to his head and pulling the trigger. We have to ask ourselves, *What is going on?*

We spend thousands of dollars on intricate object lessons and giant displays to prove exactly what the Holy Spirit and the Bible prove on their own. This book will show that the uniqueness of the church was this: evidence of the supernatural in everything they did. People have enough trouble understanding the ordinary things in life. We struggle to live in some semblance of reality because we're flooded with the spectacular and sensational everywhere we turn. Does the church really need to create its own imitation of the supernatural to get people to come and listen? Attempting to meet human need with the spectacular or outrageous may attract attention from many, but only the work of the Spirit changes lives.

Regardless of whether it's a big church, a little church, a contemporary church, a church with choirs—or a church that has a rock band and a full light show—every church demonstrating the life of Christ has within it a unique DNA. Have we lost sight of the extraordinary message and power we possess?

Think about it: Something made the original church great. It wasn't the parking, and it wasn't video clips. No, it was something in their construct, in their DNA. Regardless of size, tradition, or denomination, every fully functioning church in the world has its unique DNA. Identifying this DNA and how it makes the church unique in its power and function is the focus of this book.

I hope that as you read, you'll begin identifying with the true purpose the church has in your life—and with your role in the life of the church. I hope this book will help you find the essence of the true church within the church you already attend, or help you locate a church that exhibits the true church DNA. Using a biblical perspective to redesign our understanding of the church will free us from our existing cynicism, suspicion, and jaded tendencies. Then, hopefully, we can all find a church to attend that we're more than happy to get out of bed for.

Chapter One

WHO WOULD GOD MARRY?

I've been invited to a number of weddings recently. Do
you know what a truly single person calls a wedding? A
good Saturday ruined. No matter what your plans are, you
know they're going to be canceled because you have to go to
the wedding. So on behalf of single people everywhere, let
me say to anyone about to get married: "We're proud of you,
we're happy for you, but don't expect us to come and sit
through it. We get it; you're getting married."

I've noticed that tucked inside all the invitations I
receive, there's usually a small piece of tissue paper. I now
know it's there for all the bitter single people to wipe their
tears, because they aren't the ones getting hitched.

And why am I expected to buy a gift when I attend a
wedding? After all, it's *my* Saturday that's been ruined. I have
to ask where the couple is registered and then figure out
which pattern is the right one. Heaven forbid that the gravy
boat I buy doesn't match their teapot! (Why is it called a
gravy boat, anyway—and why do they need one?)

I'm told that appliances make good wedding gifts. Maybe that's why the toaster oven has been a mainstay in every American kitchen for the last twenty-five years. Why would anyone prefer the convenience of a microwave oven when that little toaster oven will do in forty-two minutes what a microwave can do in thirty seconds?

Then there's the crockpot. What's so special about slow-cooking your food? When I want a bowl of stew, why should I have to plan four days ahead? But my personal favorite wedding gift is the blender—because of what it says. With every blender, there's always a mishap, though. It never completely crushes the ice; the lid flies off; and there's always a mess. It's my way of saying, "Welcome to married life! Expect a life full of disappointments, unexpected problems, and other people's messes left for you to clean up." Also, the blender is good for mixing drinks. This is my way of saying, "If you're not drinking yet, you soon will be."

In all these weddings I've been attending lately, I've noticed incredible opulence. The bride and her family go to such extremes to make certain every beautiful detail is handled perfectly. Until recently I never really knew how weddings came together; I thought two people decided to get married, they told the pastor, and it all just happened.

Not so! I discovered a whole industry centered on the planning and conducting of weddings. There are bridal magazines and bridal shops. There are even schools where people can learn how to make a lot of money just putting on weddings. As a single guy, I've never really read a bridal magazine. But while researching this book, I thumbed through a couple of magazines and, frankly, I felt like I was spying on the enemy. These magazines are bursting with pictures of women wearing bridal dresses along with complete directions for where to order the one you like for the right price. I really didn't care about ordering a dress; I kept looking for the place to order the bride.

Men's experiences with weddings are really quite different from those of women. For the woman, it's the big show of her life. She gets to be front and center, forcing everyone to look at her. In a lot of ways, it's like a big, fantasy church pageant. For the man, it's more like one of those bureaucratic hoops to jump through, the red tape before hotel check-in.

When it comes to the vows, men and women hear them completely differently. A woman hears: "Do you take this man to be your lawfully wedded husband?" The guy hears: "You have the right to remain silent. Anything you say can, and will, be used against you."

> **" I really didn't care about ordering a dress; I kept looking for the place to order the bride. "**

I read an article recently about a woman who prepared an entire notebook on how she wanted her wedding to look. She had chosen the flowers, the colors, the fabrics, the lighting, and had them all laid out. The only problem was, the woman was not engaged. Now, my name isn't Dr. Date, but I'm pretty sure that to have a wedding you need some-body to marry; call me old-fashioned if you want.

Are we off topic? No. We're talking about weddings because we need to focus on the bride. The one in the Bible, that is.

One of the most important biblical images describing the church is "the bride of Christ." The more we understand this biblical portrait, the more we'll appreciate our connection to the church. You see, believers aren't isolated individuals sen-tenced to finding their own per-sonal significance in God's plan for the world. Our purpose as believers is most fully actualized as we learn to identify with the bride of Christ.

> "My name isn't Dr. Date, but I'm pretty sure that to have a wedding you need somebody to marry."

Some churches still expect worshipers to dress up, while others allow a more casual atmosphere. Some still use the pipe organ, while others have hired full-time band members for Sunday morning music. The end product is the same, regardless of the venue; people attend each type of worship experience. From my observa-tion, most churches are like middle-school students before breakfast: They stand in front of the mirror for hours, chang-ing everything from clothes to makeup, in a never-ending search for their identity. The picture of the bride is more than a symbol of how God wants the church to dress up. The bride identifies *who God has created the church to be.* Ready to look at that?

The motive of the bride is sacrifice

Every city has its own version of the Single-Mingle Publication filled with cryptic want ads from lonely people looking for other lonely people. These caught my eye:

> *Single male, thirty-something. Enjoys weightlifting and long walks on the beach. Extensive G. I. Joe collection. Call between 2 and 4 PM, when my mom is out of the house.*
>
> *Single female. Tired of Internet psychos? Do you believe fitness and dieting are overrated? Call me, 555-3663. I enjoy eating out, taking care of my cats, and eating out. A free spirit; be ready for spontaneous trips to Pigeon Forge.*
>
> *STP—Single, Tough, and Proud. Seeks woman with high teeth-to-tattoo ratio. Contact me at nascar3@nra.com.*

But if Jesus were to write an ad for his bride, it might read something like this:

> *Son of God seeks eternal bride. Pledges full inheritance to the lover of his soul. Must be willing to take on royal presence and available to carry out God's work on earth. Purpose, meaning, and power will be provided in an inexhaustible supply. Reservations already made for heavenly wedding feast.*

The Bible doesn't use abbreviations or double-speak when it describes the bride; it uses plain language. In Revelation 19:4–10, the Scripture identifies the bride in five ways, based upon the sacrifices she makes for Jesus.

The bride absolutely receives Jesus "[They] fell down and worshiped God who sits on the throne saying, 'Amen. Hallelujah!'" (v. 4). The bride completely gives herself to Jesus because she is entirely acceptable to him. Jesus sees his bride exactly as she is and intensely embraces her. The bride knows that she has been chosen and possesses nothing worthy of his attention, yet she recognizes her position and role in God's plan for the world. Worship is the bride's natural response to Jesus.

The bride glorifies the Lord, not herself "Let us rejoice and be glad and give the glory to Him, for the marriage of the Lamb has come and His bride has made herself ready" (v. 7). The bride didn't choose Jesus; she was chosen for him. He is the redeemer of the world, and the church is his eternal companion. The recovery of the world is Jesus' ongoing mission, and the church is his partner. Jesus died for the church; the church willingly lays down her life for his kingdom.

The glory is not in the conflict but in the one for whom we struggle. It is for his purpose, his kingdom, his glory that we carry out the plans and ministry of God throughout the world. He is our commander in chief, the object of our glory.

This is the natural attitude of the bride, because she knows that without the bridegroom (Jesus) there is no bride.

The bride lives to serve the Lord "It was given to her to clothe herself in fine linen ... the righteous acts of the saints" (v. 8). The life of the bride is in Jesus, and apart from him there is no life, no calling, no purpose, no identity. Everything the bride is, everything she has been called and empowered to do, is inextricably linked to Jesus. The focus of her worship is Jesus. The focus of her ministry is Jesus. The focus of her activity is Jesus. She preaches Jesus, baptizes in the name of Jesus, feeds the hungry in the name of Jesus, collects and distributes money in the name of Jesus. This is the natural response of the bride, for she realizes that serving Jesus is her essential DNA.

The bride needs to disciple the nations "'Blessed are those who are invited to the marriage supper of the Lamb.' And he said to me, 'These are true words of God'" (v. 9).

The world desperately needs Jesus. All of creation cries out for his kingdom to be as it is in heaven. The chaos and confusion of our world can only be controlled by the kingdom ethic. Thankfully, the bride has within her the burning need to spread the kingdom ethic. She accomplishes this as she disciples the nations of the world. The kingdom ethic is more than an imposed system of conditions and rules; it is the natural response of the world once it's changed by the power of God.

The bride is the dwelling place of the Spirit "I am a fellow servant of yours and your brethren who hold the testimony of Jesus" (v. 10). The Spirit of God is the living testimony of Jesus in the heart of every believer. He is no free agent, roaming about creation doing as he pleases. He inhabits the bride and carries out his work through the church. The work of the kingdom is the complete redemption of the world and is empowered by the fully functioning Spirit of God. The church is his conduit to distribute God's power throughout the world.

Can you see how the ministry of the church is much more than a well-planned worship experience on Sunday morning? The ministry of the church is flourishing when lives change, addictions break, and justice rolls like a river. A changing world proves the bride's presence, because she is the vessel of the indwelling, eternal power of God in the person of the Holy Spirit.

The embrace of the bride is service

The role of the bride of Christ has been misunderstood for too long. We have come to believe that our identity as the bride refers to who we will be in heaven when Jesus returns for the church. We have heard preachers tell us, "Jesus is coming for a spotless bride; when he comes, we must be ready." Our bridal identity is God's intentional process of leading us to assert the position he won for us on the earth. Yes, the church will be the bride of Christ in heaven, but until then, we are his bride now on the earth.

In the first century after Christ's death on the cross, the apostle John landed on the island of Patmos as an exile. He had been leading the church in Jerusalem but faced trial as an insurrectionist and was exiled. But God spoke to him in visions that he recorded in what we now have as the Book of Revelation. His words were smuggled back to the church in Jerusalem, written in language that the religious leaders would not understand but believers would.

> **Yes, the church will be the bride of Christ in heaven, but until then, we are his bride now on the earth.**

Between the years A.D. 30 and 70, the gospel of Christ was preached throughout Israel. During those years, the church experienced growing persecution from the hands of the religious elite of Jerusalem. Many believers became the targets of religious "hit men" like Saul, yet the church persevered. John's exile writings were welcomed by the church for the encouragement they brought to the church in their desperate situation.

God's plan has always included a bride for his Son; God's plan always included a church. Throughout history God has preserved a people for himself. The Old Testament is the record of God's activity in the life of Israel. Because of Abraham's faith, God chose to bless him, and the nation that arose from his descendants was Israel. I believe Israel was to be the bride of the Messiah. Because of God's continued favor, Israel became quite large and powerful, being prepared to welcome the Messiah as Jesus' bride. Israel was to be the church, but she turned her back on God and chose instead to advance her own religious kingdom rather than submit to God's plan. Therefore, Israel disqualified herself as the faithful bride of Christ.

John wrote in Revelation 19:2 that "HIS JUDGMENTS ARE TRUE AND RIGHTEOUS; for He has judged the great harlot who was corrupting the earth with her immorality, and HE HAS AVENGED THE BLOOD OF HIS BOND-SERVANTS ON HER." I believe John was telling the church that God had rejected Israel in favor of his bondservants who were coming to know Christ through the ministry of other Christians.

> **The bride is 'impregnated' with the purposes of God and births them into the world.**

This growing number of Christians is now called the church, the bride of Christ. The sanctioned bride of Christ sees her role as fulfilling the will of God on the earth. The bride is "impregnated" with the purposes of God and births them into the world. The purpose of the bride is service to the initiatives of God.

When we join a church, we are doing much more than simply adding our name to a list of people who identify with that community of faith. We take on the distinctive qualities of the bride of Christ. Don't take this lightly! These distinctions affect our attitudes, our actions, and our chosen values. We are the life partner of Jesus in the world.

The energy of the bride is supernatural

The bride functions as an army, but not an unopposed army. God does not expect us to advance the kingdom without opposition. He knows there will be opposition, and he prepares the bride with three powerful weapons for us to understand and utilize.

Praise The act of praise focuses our attention squarely on God and his activity on earth. But it's more than singing songs. It is the unity of the bride's adoration toward the One who loves her and toward his redemptive activity in the world.

I don't know why some people insist on bringing their own percussion instruments to church. I periodically attend one church that has a fantastic worship band—trust me; they don't need anyone to help. When their brass section blows, Dizzy Gillespie lifts a humble hand. But one lady in the congregation insists on bringing her own four-inch bargain Bible store tambourine with her into the pew. It's got praying hands screen-printed on the fake stretched-hide cover, and she brings it to each service, just so she can add her own special syncopated emphasis to the music. Please, all worship tambourine wannabes, you're not Thelonious Monk, so give it up and just join the bride in worship.

All forms of praise—whether in word, prayer, song, or silence—release the power of God into our lives and into the unseen reality where that power makes an eternal difference in what happens in the world. Even when we sing quiet, slow songs, God's power goes forth to accomplish his purposes.

Praise defeats our anxieties and inhibitions regarding our role in God's eternal plan. Without it, our focus naturally migrates toward our own finite abilities. We see the overwhelming task ahead of us, and our knowledge of our limitations can quickly lead us to a sense of futility. Satan knows this and does everything possible to keep us feeling despair. Praise is the weapon we use to defeat these debilitating emotions. Without praise, we could become our own worst enemy.

Prayer Simply put, prayer is conversation with God. For many, prayer has become a one-way request line. Lost are the communication skills that make prayer a dialogue. We have come to see prayer as our daily supply "order form." We properly complete the form (pray the right words) in triplicate (repeat the prayer over and over), and after a time (it usually seems too long) the Supply Sergeant (God) sends the munitions (the things we are praying for) through the proper channels (the Holy Spirit), and we receive them in the nick of time.

What a distorted and self-centered view of prayer! Our mission is God's mission, and its design is more intricate than we could ever imagine. What makes us think we even know what to "order"? Has God made us fully aware of his plans? Do we know how the actions of today will best complement tomorrow's need? "You do not have because you do not ask. You ask and do not receive, because you ask with wrong motives, so that you may spend it on your pleasures" (James 4:2–3).

I was in one church recently where a woman at prayer said, "Jesus, would you please bless God?" When I thought about what she had prayed, all I could see in my mind was Jesus listening to her prayer

> **" Do we speak respectfully of Jesus, or do we undercut his presence in our lives by drawing more attention to ourselves? "**

… when a puzzled look sets in on his face. He gets up from his intercessor's chair and scampers across the throne room, knocks on God's door, and asks, "Dad, are you alright today? Some woman just told me to come bless you. You're not holding out on me, are you?" Think about it; this is the one prayer that could bring all of heaven to a screeching halt.

Clearly, our understanding of prayer corresponds to our understanding of God. God desires to give: "Ask of God, who gives to all generously and without reproach, and it will be given" (James 1:5). And he is completely free to respond as he chooses—

> *"Or what man is there among you who, when his son asks for a loaf, will give him a stone? Or if he asks for a fish, he will not give him a snake, will he?*

*"If you then, being evil, know how to give good gifts
to your children, how much more will your Father who is
in heaven give what is good to those who ask Him!"*

—Matthew 7:9–11

When we begin to understand these things about God, we will know that we can absolutely trust him and approach prayer as a dialogue. For we are not alone in our struggle for the world. We are the channel through which God has chosen to release himself and his power into the world. We are the partner of his Son, the bride of Christ, and prayer is our line of communication. When the bride prays, awesome things happen.

Proclamation The true message of Christ is the light of the world. When we share it in clarity, and when it is empowered by the Holy Spirit, the world cannot help but understand and receive it. As the bride, we need to hear the proclamation for ourselves, of course. All persons need a pastor who will proclaim to them the thoughts and intentions God has toward them.

The other aspect of proclamation is the way the bride speaks of her beloved in her everyday life. Do we speak respectfully of Jesus, or do we undercut his presence in our lives by drawing more attention to ourselves? With our words, we are to proclaim that Jesus is alive.

Wherever I go to speak, it seems that something happens to distract me from being clear with the message of Christ. There always seems to be a problem with the lights or the microphone. Or the directions faxed to my office are wrong, or my flight is late. My personal favorite is the person who "admonishes" me just before I get up to speak. I identify these things for what they are: diversions of the Enemy attempting to make my message unclear. You see, Satan fears the clear preaching of the message of salvation because, "faith comes from hearing, and hearing by the word of Christ" (Rom. 10:17).

A friend of mine is a loan officer for a large, nationwide company. Some of the guys he works with were at lunch talking about some of the stupid things their customers did to make their job harder. Several guys traded stories, and so did my friend. One of the last to speak shared a particularly painful story, a situation in which he ended up losing quite a bit of money because of a customer's mistake. As the group groaned over the loss of money, my friend said this guy glanced at him and said, "But you know, as bad as that situation was, God reminded me that it could always be worse. I could be working at a job I hated doing." My friend told me he felt as if God's truth had been proclaimed just for him in that moment.

Whenever we proclaim the message of Christ, we unleash the living and powerful Word of God. Nothing in this world, no power or might, no person or force, can stand before the proclamation of that Word. Our message is that Christ is alive. He is the Son of God and we are his bride, bent on reclaiming the world.

The entrance of the bride is spotless

God has chosen a spotless bride for his Son. The bride was chosen and made clean by Jesus' death on the cross.

> *Just as Christ also loved the church and gave Himself up for her, so that He might sanctify her, having cleansed her by the washing of water with the word, that He might present to Himself the church in all her glory, having no spot or wrinkle or any such thing; but that she would be holy and blameless.*

—Ephesians 5:25–27

Everyone who receives Jesus as Christ and Lord is changed, born again, not of this world but of heaven. Our eternal life has already begun, and our purpose for living becomes the advancement of the kingdom of God. Our actions here on earth become the bride's heavenly gown: "It was given to her to clothe herself in fine linen, bright and clean; for the fine linen is the righteous acts of the saints" (Rev. 19:8).

❝He whispers in your ear, 'You are my delight.'❞

As the kingdom advances here on earth, heaven's bridal gown grows more beautiful and brilliant, waiting for the day when she will be presented to Christ complete in heaven. This will not take place until the end of time. But until then, the bride will continue to express her passion for Jesus, persevere in her shared mission of bringing redemption to the world—and do it all in the power of praise, prayer, and the proclamation of the gospel of peace.

In Scripture, a wedding feast illustrates "home." Imagine entering a crowded room lit with excitement, laughter, music, and the clinking of glasses. This is a homecoming like no other. As you move through the room, everyone seems to know you. As you get closer to the center of the crowd, people part and ... there he is in his beauty.

It is Jesus looking right at you.

He stretches out his hand and softly speaks. "Dance with me." You move into his arms—one hand is around your waist, the other entwined in yours—and you glide across the floor. He whispers in your ear, "You are my delight." The feast is a picture of the intimacy you have with the Lord himself. He is the bridegroom, and you are the bride. As you worship, drop your formality and look at him—the sweet and mysterious man. Receive his affirmation. Allow the words, written by a dear friend of mine, to remind you: *You are treasured.*

Home

> *My heart fails*
> *My mind falters*
> *Sometimes my passion fades*
> *Sometimes my desires change*
> *Sometimes I turn my head and look the other way.*

When I'm restless, you are rest
When I'm helpless, you are help
When I'm nervous, you settle me.
When I'm empty, you fill me
When I've gone too far, you gently bring me back home
'cause you are home.

Home is where the history begins
Home is where you delight in me
Home is where your voice is in my ear
Home is where you dance with me.

—Jami Smith

Chapter Two

WHAT'S THE DEAL WITH CHURCH PEOPLE?

In one of the noncanonical writings, there's a story about a young legal professional who was approached by Satan. The devil said, "I can arrange some things for you. I can make it so that your income increases five-fold, your partners love you, your clients love you, you have four months of vacation every year, and you'll live to be a hundred years old. The only thing I ask in return is the soul of your wife, of your children, and of *their* children—to rot in hell forever." The young lawyer sat and thought for a moment before responding: "What's the catch?"

Obviously that's a joke. And I really don't have anything against lawyers. Some of my best friends are lawyers, but in our litigious society, all of us have at least one horror story about our dealings with lawyers. I know if I were walking along the beach and saw five lawyers buried up to their necks in sand, I'd be thinking: *Somebody didn't have enough sand!*

A friend of mine had retained the services of an attorney,

but his lawyer wasn't doing what he thought was in his best interest. So he asked me if I thought he should get a different attorney. I told him, "You can if you want, but changing lawyers is like changing deck chairs on the Titanic."

The other day I was sitting under a tree in the park when I saw a lawyer and an IRS agent drowning in the lake. I knew I could only save one of them, but I couldn't decide whether to do lunch or read the paper. Speaking of the paper, I read an article the other day that the U.S. Post Office had to recall the series of stamps depicting famous lawyers because people didn't know which side of the stamp to spit on. While I sat there pondering these things, I overheard one businessman asking another, "Do you know how to get a lawyer out of a tree? Cut the rope."

Lawyers exist to make sure the party they represent doesn't get taken advantage of. They read and write documents expressing what their client wants done and the ways that action will most benefit him or her. So ... imagine if an attorney had written the Ten Commandments. Moses' famous tablets might have read something like this:

The Sovereign Almighty Creator of the Universe (hereafter known as party of the first part) does willfully and with full omniscience of all potential ramifications duly assign the ensuing commands to the rescued twelve tribes of Israel (hereafter known as the party of the second part). The People shall by all means possible, and with no room for ignorance, abide by—as well as order their individual, corporate, and family life in ways that facilitate an orderly obedience to—these commands; forthwith:

First Commandment: "You shall have no other gods before me" The party of the first part prohibits, forbids, and otherwise denies the party of the second part to select, choose, or take on any other God before him.

Second Commandment: "Make no idols" The party of the second part is prohibited from manufacturing or purchasing any premanufactured representation of gods, goddesses, or other deities. This is understood to include both animate and inanimate objects, either of which can take attention away from the party of the first part.

Third Commandment: "Do not take the name of the Lord your God in vain" The name of the party of the first part is to be held in highest regard and is to be spoken only in the deepest of reverence. All parties of the second part, as well as their descendants, shall be prohibited from conjoining the name of the party of the first part with any superfluous expletive under any circumstances whatsoever. The party of the first part is omnipresent and has omniscient awareness of every word spoken and will require that punishment be carried out upon every party of the second part who uses his name improperly.

Fourth Commandment: "Remember the Sabbath" The party of the first part, also known as Creator, does so order that the day he has deemed the Sabbath shall, at all cost, be preserved, kept, and maintained as holy, separate, and distinct from every other day. On this day the parties of the second part may not participate in the customary activities common to their everyday life, but must, in keeping with the wishes of the party of the first part, incorporate an appropriate amount of rest into this day, reflecting a desire to emulate the Creator in his agenda for the Sabbath.

Fifth Commandment: "Honor your father and your mother" The party of the first part is generous and has given the party of the second part a land that provides all their needs. Therefore it is required that honor and respect be directed toward the birth parents, or those holding the title thereof, of all parties of the second part. Failure to confer said honor is punishable by a shortening of the offender's life in the land that the party of the first part has so graciously provided.

Sixth Commandment: "Do not murder" The party of the first part is the giver of the life force enjoyed by all parties of the second part. The party of the first part is the sole owner of the authority over said life force. Under no circumstances is any party of the second part to cause to be removed the life force from any and all parties of the second part. The removal of the life force is the ultimate responsibility of the party of the first part.

Seventh Commandment: "Do not commit adultery" The party of the first part is responsible for all things bright and beautiful created in the dwelling places of the parties of the second part. However, be it understood that the party of the first part strictly prohibits all unmarried copulation among any and all parties of the second part. For underlying causes known clearly by both parties of the first and second part, such behavior is prohibited.

Eighth Commandment: "Do not steal" The party of the first part has declared it unlawful for any party of the second part to remove any possession belonging to another party of the second part without first gaining their written or verbal permission. Possession of any property of another party of the second part without said permission is considered a breach of this command.

Ninth Commandment: "Do not lie" No party of the second part is allowed to speak in a manner that is less than truthful regarding the actions, choices, or behaviors of any other party of the second part. The resulting false statements will prove injurious to the party of the second part whose actions, choices, or behaviors have been misrepresented. The party of the first part demands that all parties of the second part employ the highest modicum of decorum when articulating their opinions of all other parties of the second part.

Tenth Commandment: "Do not envy" The party of the first part expressly prohibits any party of the second part from overzealously desiring the possessions of any other party of the second part. This overzealous desire is to include the dwelling in which the party of the second part inhabits along with the spouse or marital partner who shares life with the party of the second part. It is also understood to include any and all mammals, farm or domesticated, that may share the land bearing the legal name of the party of the second part. Every party of the second part is responsible to maintain his personal desires within the boundaries of his own possessions.

Addendum to the Ten Commandments It is from this moment and forevermore required that all parties of the second part agree to binding arbitration in the case of any and all grievances encountered between them and the party of the first part. Further, the party of the first part reserves the right to appoint the arbiter of his choice in any and all episodes of arbitration. Further, the party of the first part recommends that, if any party of the second part is incapable of keeping all the aforementioned commands, the party of the second part should employ the services of Johnny Cochran.

> **When God makes an agreement, it's not to protect himself or to make sure he gets his way.**

The point of this exaggerated point is that this is *exactly the opposite* way God makes his agreements with us. When God makes an agreement, it's not to protect himself or to make sure he gets his way. Instead, he willingly binds himself and pledges his loyalty, all the while taking the risk that we might not keep our end of the contract. The new covenant is not a rigid list of dos and don'ts; rather, it is God's work of engineering and empowering humans to function in healthy and productive ways. All that we are, or ever can be, is because God has entered into an agreement to ensure that it can happen.

Every community of faith has an intrinsic identity that can be identified as the city, the bride, and the new covenant congregation. *Covenant* is a cumbersome word that simply means "agreement." It is best seen in the church which, simply put, is a group of people who have brought their lives into agreement with what God has said about them. The word *covenant* also refers to the sacred contract God made with the church.

The effect of the life of agreement is that the church is not self-stylized and doesn't create its own identity. God has already created it for us. Our identity kicks into gear as we bring our lives into full agreement with what God has said about us, the church. As we do this, we begin to live authentically according to the DNA God has placed within us.

In order to understand how the church is the covenant congregation, we must examine its individual parts. We can best observe those parts as we understand the promises God made about the church.

You see, the church has always been God's first choice. The nation of Israel was the people God chose to receive the Messiah, and he also chose those first Jewish believers to be the church, the bride, the city of faith. But when the Messiah arrived, the religious leaders denied him as the Messiah and killed him. So God then turned to the growing community of believers in Christ. This group was growing daily, as the message of Jesus spread from one person to another. Where Israel had said "No," the church said "Yes."

When the community of faith says "Yes," it defines their agreement with God. This agreement has four identifying characteristics for us to know if we are to understand our place in this agreement as the new covenant people of God.

Based on the promises of God

The first-century church was so dynamic because those early believers reached out and took ownership of the promises of God. They received the agreements the same way Abraham had: through faith. They saw the promises of God and their fulfillment in the life and work of Christ.

They found their new agreement in the Old Testament: "'Behold, days are coming,' declares the LORD, 'when I will make a new covenant with the house of Israel and with the house of Judah'" (Jer. 31:31). This is one of the first times God speaks about the new covenant community, and it serves as the foundation of the church's identification and claim to the authority and power of God. It is the promise of God that gives legitimacy to the church to this very day.

But lest you think it's merely an Old Testament concept, quickly check out these New Testament verses:

- Luke 22:20. [Jesus said]: "This cup which is poured out for you is the new covenant in My blood."
- 1 Corinthians 11:25. In the same way He took the cup also after supper, saying, "This cup is the new

covenant in My blood; do this, as often as you
drink it, in remembrance of Me."

- 2 Corinthians 3:6. Who also made us adequate as servants of a new covenant, not of the letter but of the
Spirit; for the letter kills, but the Spirit gives life.
- Hebrews 8:8. Finding fault with [the first covenant],
He says, "Behold, days are coming," says the Lord,
"when I will effect a new covenant with the house of
Israel and with the house of Judah." (Also see Heb.
8:13; 9:15.)

When He said, "A new covenant," He has made the first
obsolete. But whatever is becoming obsolete and growing old
is ready to disappear ... . And for this reason, He is the mediator of a new covenant. Since a death has taken place for the
redemption of the transgressions that were committed under
the first covenant, those who have been called may receive
the promise of the eternal inheritance.

- Hebrews 12:24. To Jesus, the mediator of a new
covenant, and to the sprinkled blood, which
speaks better than the blood of Abel.

God makes a promise that he will place his identifying
DNA in their hearts: "I will put My law within them and on
their heart I will write it; and I will be their God, and they
shall be My people" (Jer. 31:33). This promise is that we will
not have to wonder about our identity or how we are to live.
As we live our lives in agreement with God and his plans for

life, our natural behavior will cooperate with his continuing work to redeem the world.

God also promises to do an internal work of forgiveness. No longer would temple sacrifices be needed: "They will not teach again, each man his neighbor and each man his brother, saying, 'Know the LORD,' for they will all know Me, from the least of them to the greatest of them," declares the LORD, "for I will forgive their iniquity, and their sin I will remember no more" (Jer. 31:34). The sacrifice of his Son, Jesus, would once and for all cover the sins of those who come to him as Christ and Lord. The external symbols were abolished because the inner work was complete.

The presence of God comes to live inside of us in the person of the Holy Spirit. "'I will be a father to you, and you shall be sons and daughters to Me,' says the Lord Almighty" (2 Cor. 6:18). We become his children, and he becomes our Father. Our ultimate identity comes through in these verses. He is our Father, he promises full and complete salvation, he promises the life of the Spirit living within us, and the Spirit of God will teach us how to make sense of all this.

> **❝I hope it's becoming clear to you: The church is not a product of man-made ideas.❞**

I hope it's becoming clear to you: The church is not a product of man-made ideas; it is formed out of God's self-motivated new covenant. Many of us have belonged to churches that talk about the new covenant God made with us, but they do it in an old-covenant way. Their message is, "He has removed our sins, he lives inside of us, and here are the lists of dos and don'ts he expects us to keep." At first sight, this message seems to support the new covenant, right? Yet the rules that follow reveal a lack of belief to truly trust it and live it out in daily life.

The members of the new covenant congregation have found their new identity in Christ, who resides in them. When they speak of being Christian, they aren't talking about the relative virtue of their behaviors or how long it's been since they did something that displeased God. They're speaking about who the new covenant says they are.

When we give our lives to Christ, we become a new people, the sons and daughters of God. Our identity stands upon these four promises of the new covenant community, not upon how well we live up to any list of behaviors, regardless of how good or well-meaning the list may be.

We can enter into the presence of God because of the new covenant. No longer do we need a priest to make sacrifices for us, because the ultimate sacrifice (Christ) lives in our hearts. No longer do we need a priest to intercede for us; Jesus is our advocate, and he sits at the Father's right hand.

Think about what this can mean to a church! We are not just a gathering of individuals. No, we're a unified congregation in possession of a new covenant. We understand who we are in Christ, and we live out our lives in agreement with the promises God made to us. Together we worship and actually enter the presence of God. When we do, we truly experience the presence of God in the way he intended.

Become new people

Ready to hear more about your true identity? Drink it in ...

> *"Then I Myself will gather the remnant of My flock out of all the countries where I have driven them and bring them back to their pasture, and they will be fruitful and multiply. I will also raise up shepherds over them and they will tend them; and they will not be afraid any longer, nor be terrified, nor will any be missing," declares the LORD. "Behold, the days are coming," declares the LORD, "when I will raise up for David a righteous Branch; and He will reign as king and act wisely and do justice and righteousness in the land. In His days Judah will be saved, and Israel will dwell securely; and this is His name by which He will be called, 'The LORD our righteousness.'"*
>
> —Jeremiah 23:3–6

In the Old Testament, God identifies the members of the new covenant congregation. In the New Testament, he calls it the church. The verses above mention gathering a *remnant;* these are the believing Jews and Gentiles. The righteous Branch he will raise up is Jesus, who will bring righteousness and justice. Paul provides further insight in the New Testament:

> *"I will call those who were not My people, 'My people,' and her who was not beloved, 'beloved.' And it*

shall be that in the place where it was said to them,
'You are not My people,' there they shall be called sons
of the living God ... Though the number of the sons of
Israel be like the sand of the sea, it is the remnant that
will be saved."

—Romans 9:25–27

This is the new covenant community. It's not about behavior or levels of moral advancement. Those who open their lives to Christ ... are in. God calls people from all parts of the earth to come and be a part. Every Old Testament promise comes to pass in this new congregation. God is creating a mosaic of people from every tribe, tongue, and nation who are willing to believe in Christ.

> **"God is creating a mosaic of people from every tribe, tongue, and nation who are willing to believe in Christ."**

This is the reason every church is different. More than one kind of person goes to church, and no style of worship and ministry fits everyone. But regardless of style, size, or brand, every church effectively demonstrating the life of Christ will display diversity. God is making a mosaic, a beautiful pattern, a patchwork of a new race of people on the earth called the new covenant congregation.

Built through power

God gives the new congregation power to bind and loose, to forbid and permit. So this congregation has awesome power, but it acts only under the obedience of Christ Jesus.

> *He said to them, "But who do you say that I am?"*
> *Simon Peter answered, "You are the Christ, the Son of the*
> *living God."*
>
> *And Jesus said to him, "Blessed are you, Simon*
> *Barjona, because flesh and blood did not reveal this to*
> *you, but My Father who is in heaven. I also say to you*
> *that you are Peter, and upon this rock I will build My*
> *church; and the gates of Hades will not overpower it. I*
> *will give you the keys of the kingdom of heaven; and*
> *whatever you bind on earth shall have been bound in*
> *heaven, and whatever you loose on earth shall have been*
> *loosed in heaven."*
>
> —Matthew 16:15–19

Can you see that the power of the kingdom has been given to us in the congregation? We are not the kingdom; we *release* the kingdom. The rule of Christ created this new covenant congregation, and the power he gives to this new community is to represent the King throughout the earth. No single individual believer has the power; instead, *the entire congregation has power.* The power comes from the King and comes to us only as we represent him on the earth.

What kind of power is it? Consider this: "Jesus summoned His twelve disciples and gave them authority over unclean spirits, to cast them out, and to heal every kind of disease and every kind of sickness" (Matt. 10:1). It is the power to cast out and to heal. This shouldn't frighten us, but it does. Everywhere I've preached this point, the people in the room seem startled at my words. But I'm not making this stuff up. This is the power Jesus gives to the new covenant congregation.

There's more. "As you go, preach, saying, 'The kingdom of heaven is at hand'" (Matt. 10:7). When the world hears this, they instantly hear, "The end of the world is near," and they quickly equate the speaker with the stereotypical bearded, rag-clothed man on the streets holding a placard bearing the same words. They don't realize what this statement is saying, though—that the kingdom is about to advance into their lives.

Think about it. Wherever we go, we carry with us the ability to cast out, and heal, and expand the kingdom of God. Does the kingdom of God need to expand into and throughout your office? Does it need to permeate your school or university? Does it need to come alive in power within your home? Wherever you go, preach the message with your life that the kingdom of heaven is at hand.

"He who receives you receives Me, and he who receives Me receives Him who sent Me" (Matt. 10:40). When we live in agreement with the will of God for our world, we should have a confident recognition of who we are. The reactions and responses of people are completely irrelevant. When they receive you, they are being receptive to Jesus. When they push you away, they are pushing Jesus away. When they receive Jesus, they are receiving the King of the Universe into their lives. What a great calling we have! What a great way to look at our activities in the world!

> **The church's focus on keeping the rules is simply an attempt at godliness through behavior modification.**

We must live with a more practical view of eternity because the life of every person on earth is at stake. What I'm about to write is extremely radical and non-postmodern, but there's no pastel way to deliver this truth. Jesus is saying that if people don't receive us, they are not receiving Jesus, and they will be judged. "When the Son of Man comes in His glory, and all the angels with Him, then He will sit on His glorious throne" (Matt. 25:31). Jesus gives us real power to make a difference upon the earth. We are to live out the kingdom presence in the world, taking with us the covenant message. This is Christ's mission lived out on earth; it is the definition of our DNA. "When He had said this, He breathed on them and said to them, 'Receive the Holy Spirit. If you forgive the sins of any, their sins have been forgiven them; if you retain the sins of any, they have been retained'" (John 20:22–23). In other words, we have the power to loose and to bind.

And be clear about this: Jesus isn't calling us to try and be better people. The church's focus on keeping the rules is simply an attempt at godliness through behavior modification. This is one of the primary distractions keeping us from accepting the power Christ has given the church. That power is not for making us better, nicer, cuter, happier people with more knowledge. The church is to have an actual say in establishing the direction of the world. This power is to enable us to demonstrate and expand the kingdom of God in our lives.

We are representatives of the kingdom presence on the earth. We are not people sent out on our own terms to produce our own freedom. We are sent out with the power of Christ to live on his terms. Sadly, however, the church has become afraid to call believers to Christ's higher standards. Instead, we have lowered the bar and settled for just keeping a few rules.

The call of this chapter is to rise up and take on the kingdom initiative. Take on the power God has made available to us through the new covenant. Use that power to pray for people and speak to them on the behalf of God. And why shouldn't we do this? After all, what we offer, every person needs. We offer them the only way they are able to possess eternal life.

Brings purpose

When we understand the power of agreement and what it means to join the covenant community, we will see that our participation is more than a formality; it is planting our "yes" into a local congregation. The result is a composite "yes" of the congregation that empowers the church's activities in the world. Because the power of a community brought into agreement will come through in its actions. This community becomes a conduit, distributing the life of Christ throughout the earth. The believers become the way the world sees Jesus. In the words of Scripture, here's how that community will look:

They're led by the Spirit of God "All who are being led by the Spirit of God, these are sons of God" (Rom. 8:14). When the Spirit of God leads us, we learn to know the desires of God in specific situations. We begin to sense his still, small voice, and we trust he's guiding us. Knowing his purposes, we become comfortable incorporating them into our daily activities.

They're aggressively serving the King "YOU SHALL WORSHIP THE LORD YOUR GOD, AND SERVE HIM ONLY" (Matt. 4:10). Worship becomes much more than an activity relegated to one morning each week. And service transcends even "church work." Both become a passion that invades every aspect of life.

They're bringing esteem to God "That with one accord you may with one voice glorify the God and Father of our Lord Jesus Christ" (Rom. 15:6). Agreement with each other, sharing the same mindset about the spreading of his purposes in the world, brings esteem to God. Hypocrisy is the self-serving motivation that sidetracks the church from maximizing its impact on the world. Eliminating hypocrisy is the same as erasing the self-serving motive of our hearts. This results in the rapid deployment of God's purpose and the extreme esteem of God.

They live ordered lives "Therefore do not let sin reign in your mortal body so that you obey its lusts" (Rom. 6:12). This verse is about purity. The way we order our lives is either pure or it's not. But purity means more than living by an acceptable code of behavior. It's more than signing a commitment to avoid specific vices. It is living a life that is *purely in sync with the purpose of God*. According to this verse, we clearly have the choice as to what will rule our mortal bodies. The challenge is to realize that our bodies are like a clear plastic bottle. The contents are easily seen through our actions and attitudes; in other words, what's on our insides produces the things others see in us. We are called to order the inside things purely. When we do, the outside things will be easier to control.

They demonstrate self-control "Do not go on presenting the members of your body to sin as instruments of unrighteousness; but present yourselves to God as those alive from the dead, and your members as instruments of righteousness to God" (Rom. 6:13). This is the great challenge of agreement: Not to waste our lives on things that steal our kingdom productivity. Instead, we're called to present our lives to God as if dead to our own willful desires. These desires only produce works that enhance our own existence. Rather, we demonstrate that we have gained a measure of control over our body and soul such that we become instruments in his hands. The opposition of all unrighteousness is more than overt warfare. Many times we oppose unrighteousness simply by doing the good work of God in the world.

They're committed to global Christianization "Go therefore and make disciples of all the nations ... teaching them to observe all that I commanded you" (Matt. 28:19–20).

Obviously, we ought to help other people come into the same agreement with the life of Christ that we share. A disciple knows that "all I have commanded you" is about this agreement. Global Christianization happens when individuals connect their lives with Christ and find their place in the community of Christ.

As communities all over the globe begin to say "yes" to the Lord, then the parts of the world that need the changes of God are made available to the infiltration of this new covenant congregation. Being a "church person" means more than just having your name on the role and making token attempts to attend. Real "church people" move into the world, having said "yes" to him with their lives. They carry with them Christ's assurance that he is ever in agreement with them.

"I am with you always, even to the end of the age."
—Matthew 28:20

Chapter Three

DID I GET OUT OF BED FOR THIS?

I f personal success is to have ultimate meaning, then we must understand the role of the church in our lives. God is the life-giver, and he gives life through Jesus; therefore, Jesus is the source of the church. If we are to succeed in *life*, we must understand *church-life*.

The primary channel by which believers connect with God is the church. Only through this connection do we have relevance in the world. In fact, this is always God's order of things: First he does the work in the church, and then he uses the church to do his work in the world.

So what is God doing in the church these days? I believe he's building an entirely new culture within it. And it's not just a culture of skits, cool music, entertainment, and anecdotes. No, he's building something that will impact the entire cosmos, and his plans for this new culture include every believer. This means God has work to do in all of us, work that can't be done in isolation; it requires our regular involvement in the church community.

Most of the promises throughout Scripture speak to the whole community of faith rather than just individuals. This may shock you, but most of those promises can *only* be claimed by believers who are properly related to the church. Believers' lives are falling apart because they have a relationship with God, but they aren't properly related to the community of faith. God never intended Christianity to be an individual journey for lone rangers. That's why he provided the church.

In Revelation 21, we read about "the city of God." A reference to heaven? No, it describes the church and its ultimate identification. The city of God, the new Jerusalem, and the heavenly Jerusalem all describe the church as God designed it to be—full of greatness and glory. Of course, we shouldn't view the city of God as a building with a steeple on top, filled with ornate artwork and opulence. Nor is it something that looks like a well-maintained health facility. Rather, it resembles ... *a city!*

We'll need to deconstruct some of our opinions of the church if we're to take up a new understanding of it. And we must be willing to overlook past and present church experiences in order to accomplish this. Are you willing to do that? If so, you'll enter a fresh, new point of view that, I believe, better accords with the biblical view.

Four qualities of the church will help us begin to see it as a city.

The city has great significance

To understand the significance of the city of God, we first need to understand that the first heaven and the first earth had passed away: "Then I saw a new heaven and a new earth; for the first heaven and the first earth passed away, and there is no longer any sea" (Rev. 21:1).

Let me suggest an interpretation here: This "first" was the Old Agreement, the community of faith God had made with Moses (for a fuller explanation of this subject, please read my book "The God of Yes"). With this passing away, Christ now brings a new community into the world. It is through this new community, this city, that the work of God will be done in the earth.

> **The church isn't a man-made society that has somehow earned God's stamp of approval. It is a city that has its origins in heaven.**

The church isn't a man-made society that has somehow earned God's stamp of approval. It is a city that has its origins in heaven. The church is to be the earthly demonstration of God's heavenly city. "I saw the holy city, new Jerusalem, coming down out of heaven from God" (Rev. 21:2). The significance of the city is that it is first heavenly and then earthly, an extension of the city that has been built in heaven. It has the same construction blueprint.

The city of God is alive with the cooperation of all its citizens, each working together to accomplish the work of God. The success of the city depends on the vitality of its individual parts. No part can exist independent from the others. This community spirit that fills the heavenly city is the template for the church. The church is the city of God on earth, and we are the citizens who work together to accomplish his will "on earth as it is in heaven."

We all have a concept of a city of people who work together. The government works with the citizens, businesses work with the suppliers and sell to buyers, all the streets ultimately connect, and the result is that the city grows. The significance of identifying the church as the city is this: It has the infrastructure of heaven. In other words, the church is to function the same way as heaven does.

Along with these aspects of significance is this key truth: The city is the dwelling place of God. "I heard a loud voice from the throne, saying, 'Behold, the tabernacle of God is among men, and He will dwell among them, and they shall be His people, and God Himself will be among them'" (Rev. 21:3). This verse tells us that God dwells in this city. Now, we receive the presence of Christ at the moment we open our lives to him in being born again. But the dwelling place of God, the full council of God, does not reside in us individually. Instead, this can only be actualized through our collective participation in the community of faith.

> **"Our generation has the idea that we will come to Jesus and do our own thing."**

Think about how practical and encouraging that is! There are times when the things going on in my life are more than I can handle alone; I need the church. The same is true in every life. We all need the full council of God found only in the church, the city of God. Many people never realize the full power of the presence of God because they are not properly related to the church. Make no mistake, God dwells in his city, the church. And the church is the place to experience God's fullness completely.

Our generation has the idea that we will come to Jesus and do our own thing. If the church works into that, fine. If not, that's alright too. We have come to see the church as an option, almost as an opponent to personal spiritual fulfillment. In fact, many people say they want Jesus, but they don't want anything to do with the church. I've seen people sign up for missions and other great humanitarian projects and then heard them say, "I want to know Jesus and make a difference in the world, but I don't need the church to do that."

Can you now see how impossible that is? It's weird-o-rama! The significance of the church *requires* that we understand this: It is impossible to be "pro-God" and "anti-church." The truth is, for every one of us, the success of our lives will be discovered inside the city of God.

The city has a solid standard

This is the critical question: Who gets to be a part of the city? Answer: Only new people get to be a part of the city, not old people. But it has nothing to do with age. That is, only people who've been made new by the life of Christ get to be a part of the city; therefore, new life in Christ is the standard of the city. This means your personal encounter with Christ determines your citizenship.

And you'll want to be a citizen, for "He will wipe away every tear from their eyes; and there will no longer be any death; there will no longer be any mourning, or crying, or pain; the first things have passed away" (Rev. 21:4). These words are all about the church. John penned the Book of Revelation as the church faced extreme persecution. Believers were being burned and skinned alive, drawn and quartered, fed to the lions. John received word of these things even while exiled on the island of Patmos.

During these dark days, John wrote to the believers that there was a newness coming, that God was making all things new. The Romans destroyed the old city of Jerusalem in A.D. 70, and now God was creating a new city, the community of faith. Through this great new community, God would release himself and his power into dominance throughout the world.

The new life we receive at the moment of trusting Jesus can't be lived in isolation. That life is only fully actualized in the context of the community of faith. When we are tormented by the past, we remember our new identity within the context of the church. Just as the early believers were persecuted, we, too, face opposition because of our faith. It could come from our own wrong choices or our past mistakes. But when we feel the pain, we remember our citizenship in the new city.

Left on our own, we are trapped in the old way of living. But through Christ and our connection to the church, we find our full expression as citizens in the city of God. This is the only context in which we can see ourselves as we truly are, the sons and daughters of God. That's why I emphasize: The standard of the city is the presence of the life of Christ.

The city has a definite structure

How is the city set up? Think about this verse for a moment: "'Bring the whole tithe into the storehouse, so that there may be food in My house, and test Me now in this,' says the LORD of hosts, 'if I will not open for you the windows of heaven and pour out for you a blessing until it overflows'" (Mal. 3:10).

It's no accident that the Bible compares the church with a city, because every city requires its citizens to fund its function. The same is true with the church. When we are faithful in our support of the city of God, the dividends of God flow back into the church.

But what about the *individuals* who make up the city of God? As individual citizens, aren't we entitled to receive God's return dividends? The answer is a qualified yes. As long as we remain properly related to the city of God, we will receive the individual benefit of the

> **❝Once we understand that the full life of God blossoms in the church, we'll want to be part of that body. ❞**

corporate dividend of God. Jesus promised his presence

wherever "two or three" were gathered together in his name. When he was leaving earth to return to heaven, he told his disciples, "I am with you [collectively] always." The dividends of God are given to the city of God, and we realize the benefit of these dividends as citizens of his city.

Please realize that going to heaven is not only an individual matter. It is a corporate event as well. That is, the church is going to heaven. "Just Jesus and me" really isn't a biblical idea. In fact, it's kind of an idolatrous concept—you are the worshiper, bowing down to an image that looks ... just like yourself! Nowhere does the Bible teach that it's just Jesus and me; it's always Jesus in the context of his bride, the city of God, the church.

> **"Do we focus on how our ministry makes us look—rather than how it makes him look?"**

In Mark 6:7, Jesus gave his disciples his authority and paired them up to send them into the community. In verse 13 of that same chapter, we read that the disciples cast out demons and healed many sick people. Pay particular attention here: They weren't *individually* doing these things; they were in pairs. They went corporately, in groups of two, to carry out the Lord's work.

Once we truly grasp the biblical concept of the church, we'll realize the significance of our part in the church. Once we understand that the full life of God blossoms in the church, we'll want to be part of that body. We'll walk into a local church and say, "I can see the city of God in this community of faith." When we understand the significance, the standard, and the structure of the city of God, the church begins to make much more sense.

The city has a stunning success

Revelation 21:9 through 22:5 is all about the success of the city. Here is a glimpse of it:

> *Then one of the seven angels who had the seven bowls full of the seven last plagues came and spoke with me, saying, "Come here, I will show you the bride, the wife of the Lamb." And he carried me away in the Spirit to a great and high mountain, and showed me the holy city, Jerusalem, coming down out of heaven from God, having the glory of God. Her brilliance was like a very costly stone, as a stone of crystal-clear jasper.*
>
> —Revelation 21:9–11

Read those verses again and take in the beauty of the city of God. The whole concept and dynamic of church is much more than our Sunday morning programs. It is larger than our budgets and building programs. John's vision goes far beyond the one who preaches in a pulpit, or who leads the worship, or who teaches a class, or even who sings solos in the Easter musical. John says the brilliance of the city was harder to describe than the largest, most beautiful diamond ever seen by human eyes. This stunning city was built at the expense of the blood of Jesus. I have to ask the question, then: Is what we do as a church worthy of the price God paid for it?

For example, do we focus on how our ministry makes us look—rather than how it makes him look? We seem to be satisfied when our parking lots are full. We judge the success of a summer camp by the number of campers. If we have to add chairs for the Christmas program, then the program was a success. If the offering totals what it did during the same week last year, then everything is fine. We'll do just about anything it takes to keep the attendance strong and growing, even if it means the content we present is weak. And so many of our churches focus on fitting into the culture rather than changing the culture around them.

In Revelation 21 and 22, we read of high walls surrounding the city of God. These walls provide security for the citizens, who won't have to suffer anymore. In Revelation 21:15, a golden measuring rod shows the size of the city: 1,500 miles long; 1,500 miles wide; 1,500 miles high. That's 1,500 cubic miles of city.

Now 1,500 miles is about the length of a straight line from St. Louis to Los Angeles. Can you imagine how many people it will take to populate a *cubic* city this size? This is God's way of measuring the success of his city. This is the place Jesus left to prepare for us (see John 14:2). It is overwhelming! It is expansive! This city isn't just a little town stuck somewhere on the outskirts of the universe. The city of God is where the church of the ages will be united and live under the reign of Jesus.

John pictures a shiny, shimmering place: "The material of the wall was jasper; and the city was pure gold, like clear glass" (Rev. 21:18). Imagine, if you can, that God is building his kingdom in the 1,500-cubic-mile area—that's 1,500 miles north and south, east and west, and 1,500 miles straight up. In order for a city

> " It is overwhelming! It is expansive! This city isn't just a little town stuck somewhere on the outskirts of the universe. "

this size to be filled with people, the kingdom of God must have enormous impact on the earth. This city wasn't built to be a ghost town; it was built to teem with throngs of peoples from all nations. And God didn't make any mistake in laying out the dimensions here. He built this city to exact size, perfect for those who would inhabit it.

Are you beginning to see it? The impact the church will have on the earth is nearly immeasurable. This city glistens with the light of God (v. 23), and the world will see how to walk by the light emanating through its walls (v. 24). This world is lost without the city of God, for everything else is darkness.

But let's thoughtfully ask ourselves: Is the culture surrounding the church being changed? Are the citizens of the city of God affecting the way people think and live? That should be happening, because the water of life runs through the center of the city. "He showed me a river of the water of life, clear as crystal, coming from the throne of God and of the Lamb, in the middle of its street" (Rev. 22:1–2).

The river represents the impact of the church upon society. God's plan is for the church to release life and healing throughout the world, for the church is God's redemptive agent in our culture. This river originates from the unlimited supply of the throne of God, and the world desperately needs everything God supplies. The city is the conduit God has chosen to deliver this healing.

If we are to deliver everything God has for the world, we must be a committed and confident people. We must function as fully endowed citizens in complete cooperation with God's reclamation of the world. Thus the world will say: "Sign us up! Let's get ourselves to the city!"

Bottom line: Church effectiveness has little to do with parking spaces and budget figures. No, it's about the city of God and *the flow of its river of life into the world.* We need to encourage the flow through us. When this becomes our focus, we'll begin to hear the world around us saying, "We need your waters; we need the healing you have." When this becomes our focus, church will become something of importance, something of power. And we'll be more than glad that we got out of bed for it.

Chapter Four

WHY CAN'T I TiVo CHURCH?

Most people have a story of attending a church that has, in some way, disappointed them. These memories then function as the standard against which all other churches get measured. But this comparison method is unfair, because all churches have their special ways of doing things. The real problem is that you may have just been in the wrong church. And there are ways to know if you are, indeed, in that difficult situation.

You may be in the wrong church if ...
- the communion cups have salt around the rims;
- the church bus sports a gun rack;
- the offering plates have charge-card slots;
- the pews have built-in 32-oz. cupholders;
- the choir wears Hooters t-shirts instead of robes;
- the call to worship song is "Born to Be Wild";
- the communion wafers are deep fried;
- people are seated based on their year-to-date giving;
- the church bookstore sells Christian thongs;

- the missions team "ministers" in Vegas ... three times a year.

When we use bad church experiences of the past to determine our future attendance, we're really starting off on the wrong foot. Maybe we ought to exchange our current stencil for a biblical model of what going to church is all about.

The act of going to church encompasses more than simply traveling to a building to spend an hour with other Christians. Most of the time, we haven't thought about the value of going to a place to meet God. When we're on our way to church, we're often completely preoccupied with our personal agendas. Many of us are still trying to rub the club stamps off our wrists from the night before. Others are running traffic lights, hoping to enter the service before that "fashionably late" bell rings.

I hear people say, "The church is not a building." But don't we usually picture it as a building because that's the place where we meet? We say, "We're going to church," or "The church at Second and Broadway is where I attend." Throughout Christian history, there was always a place where God's people met. Even in the New Testament, they gathered from house to house.

Here's my point: God dwells in believers, and we individually know him within the intimate setting of our own lives. But when individual believers come together in one place, it is in that setting that we fully experience the Lord. We are his sanctuary, his church; we are together, and he inhabits his sanctuary. If we survey the Scripture looking for references to the church as a sanctuary, we'll find several important aspects worth noting.

The sanctuary is unique

The primary reason the church is unique is because it is the sanctuary, the dwelling place of God: "I will place them and multiply them, and will set My sanctuary in their midst forever" (Ezek. 37:26). The style or cost of a church building is irrelevant. The color of carpets or number of floors in the educational building matters little compared to the inherent value every church possesses as God's dwelling place.

But have we lost sight of exactly who awaits us as we park our cars and enter the building we call the church? The familiarity of our fellowship, the predictability of our worship, and the comfortable sameness, week after week, seems to have lulled us into a sense that nothing really special is happening in our meetings. We dutifully fulfill our church-going habit, hardly realizing just how unique the experience truly is. It is in the sanctuary that we realize God's tranquility, God's triumph, and our togetherness with God. When we ourselves thrill to this uniqueness of the sanctuary, the world will take notice and long to join us.

Jesus took the twelve disciples with him everywhere he went. They watched him as he taught and healed the sick. Whether or not they knew it, while they were with Jesus, he was teaching them about the pattern of the church. When he and the twelve met together, they were having church. When he sent them out in pairs, they went out as the church. In Matthew 18:20 when he said, "For where two or three have gathered together in My name, I am there in their midst," he was teaching church. The church originated with Jesus. It is his unique plan to share his life with the world.

The sanctuary must be understood

God has forever tied his presence to the sanctuary, the church, the place where he connects with his people. But how, exactly, does God make his presence known to us?

Realize that the tabernacle is a type and shadow of the church. While Israel was on the move through the wilderness, God's presence went before the people, in cloud by day and as a pillar of fire by night. When they stopped to set up camp, they immediately set up the portable tabernacle, the place God came to dwell. The tabernacle was a literal structure with a spiritual analogy. God uses the tabernacle to teach us the pattern of our entire life in him.

When the tabernacle was set up, God would enter into the sanctuary, a large, ornate tent. Surrounding this tent was a portable wall made of thick cloth draped over poles that stood in bases. The space between the wall and the sanctuary was called the *inner court,* and only the priests could enter

> **God uses the tabernacle to teach us the pattern of our entire life in him.**

that area. Beyond and surrounding this boundary was another temporary wall enclosing the *outer court*. Here the worshiper would enter to bring a sacrifice. The priests would meet worshipers in the outer court and carry their sacrifices into the inner court.

Inside the sanctuary was a smaller room also separated by heavy curtains. This room was the Holy of Holies and was the resting place of the Ark of the Covenant (the sacred chest holding Aaron's rod that budded, a golden pot of manna, and the two tablets of the Ten Commandments). God would come to dwell in the Holy of Holies. Once this room was set up and God's presence had come inside, no one but the high priest was allowed to enter that room.

When God came into the tabernacle, I believe the Holy of Holies would literally glow with his presence. The invisible glory of God became visible through the thick curtains of the physical structure. God was in the sanctuary.

Beyond the temporary walls of curtains, the Hebrew people lived and carried on their business. The walls provided a visible separation between them and God, but they also represented a spiritual separation. In other words, every individual lived just outside the presence of God. The Almighty lived *in* his sanctuary, and they lived *around* the sanctuary. They could see the glow of God's presence, they knew he was there, but they required a priest to be their mediator with God. The priest would receive their sacrifices and offerings and take them before God. Without the priest, the individual had no connection with God.

In 1 Chronicles, Solomon builds a permanent temple. His father, David, had designed it and raised much of the money to build it, but Solomon erected it. Construction of the temple lasted seven years, and it took another thirteen years to decorate. When completed, the dedication ceremony included a spectacular demonstration no one could have expected. The house filled with a thick cloud of God's presence, and no one was able to stand. God's presence was so real, so complete, that everyone there had to kneel.

This was the same basic temple layout that Jesus visited every time he was in Jerusalem. Within the outer walls of this temple was the outer court, and inside that was another wall that separated the outer court from the inner court. And inside that wall was the sanctuary and the Holy of Holies. Obviously, this permanent temple followed the pattern of the portable tabernacle Israel had used in the wilderness. For centuries, people would bring their sacrifices and offerings to the temple. And priests still served as messengers between the individual and God, for God was still within his sanctuary.

But on the day Jesus went to the cross ... everything changed forever. During Jesus' execution, the sky turned dark. At that exact moment, the thick curtain, or veil, separating the Holy of Holies from the rest of the nation was torn in half, from the top to the bottom (see Matt. 27:51; Luke 23:45). This was God's way of saying: "I have now changed my address!" From now on, his sanctuary would be the lives of those who had come to know Jesus as Christ and Lord.

Jesus himself became the High Priest who lives within us. In him, then, we have complete access to God *because we have become his sanctuary.*

Where is God today? Some believe they've discovered him while meditating in the mountains. Others think they find him while making dream catchers in Santa Fe. Still others claim their God-discovery while in Montreal making candles. These locations and experiences may bring individuals a sense of transcendence. And this, of course, can aid in the human search for God. But God himself is, and always has been, in the sanctuary.

> **The suggestion that believers don't need a physical gathering place is an American idea—that we can find God wherever we want to find him and worship him in any way we choose.**

The suggestion that believers don't need a physical gathering place is an American idea—that we can find God wherever we want to find him and worship him in any way we choose. I saw a guy wearing a T-shirt displaying a bed with this caption: "Worship God on Sunday morning." This idea has saturated America. We do the Sunday-morning rollover at Bedside Baptist. Pastor Pillow and Deacon Sheets are there to comfort us. Or we click on a TV preacher and think we've done church, because we can be with God wherever we are.

This is just not true. God has a dwelling place. It is called the local church, and he directs all believers to be united with it. In 1 Peter 2:5, the Bible says that in Christ all of us have become "living stones," and we are being built together into a "holy house," or the new dwelling place for God. We bear the address of God on our lives. If someone has the life of Christ within him and is *not* connected together with other believers in a local community, then he is a stone out of place. His witness is just as effective as a brick lying beside the road.

> **When somebody says she's a church member, it could mean almost anything these days.**

No! We are living stones, re-created to bond together and form the dwelling place of God.

There is a need in America, and it is a need for the house of God. There is a need in the church of America, and it is a need for the renewed commitment to be continually becoming the dwelling place of God. When the believers of America see themselves as the new sanctuary of God, unique and powerful things take place.

The whole point is this: God dwells in community. When the Israelites set up the tabernacle in the wilderness, they would place it in the center of their camp. Years later, when they had come to dwell in the Holy Land, the worship center for each town was built in the middle of the village. The message is: God dwells in community. It's not just a building; it's the place where God dwells with his people.

The sanctuary must be utilized

God has promised his presence among his people. And God is never without authority and power. Yet his power and authority is often never utilized, or it is underutilized.

I'd like to explain this by first asking: Are you beginning to see the historic connection between the sanctuary of the Old Testament and the present-day church? The Bible puts it like this: "So then you are no longer strangers and aliens, but you are fellow citizens with the saints, and are of God's household, having been built on the foundation" (Eph. 2:19–20).

Think about the role of these citizens for a moment. Believers are not just *members* of a church, they are an integral part of the *structure*. The church cannot exist without the citizens any more than it can exist without the presence of God. It is the presence of God that gives believers their identity as the church, and it is the unified operation of believers in the world that give substance to God's presence in the world. When people come into the kingdom of God, they are no longer strangers or aliens; they join the ranks of the saints and citizens. We are the people of God in his dwelling place.

When somebody says she's a church member, it could mean almost anything these days. To some people, it means they signed a card at that building when they were a child. To others, it means they gave money to a particular budget. Some people think that if they attend church twice a month it makes them a member.

The term *member* usually means paying dues, passing an entrance exam, or simply being accepted as a part of the regular group. The benefits of membership? You get to attend events, help with planning, and share some responsibilities. A member can easily pay her dues, attend a couple of meetings, and fulfill her obligations to maintain her membership status. At the same time, she can just as easily move her membership to another group with little sense of loss. Or she can completely withdraw from participating in any such organization.

The term *citizen*, however, bears a permanent meaning. As citizens of the church, we are much more than names on a roster. We are legal operatives of the ongoing work being performed in heaven. The foundation of God's will has been established in heaven, and we are integrated as citizens into this extension of heaven on earth. Our role as citizens is to bring into life the kingdom of God and his will.

Can you see that we must change our understanding of church membership? Our participation in church far exceeds Sunday morning worship attendance. It bypasses our consistent financial contributions. These are external evidences of an eternal identity. The better we understand our citizenship in earth's physical extension of heaven's work, the more meaning will flow into our worship, and the more fulfillment we will know as we continue giving our time and resources.

We are being built into the dwelling place of God, "having been built on the foundation of the apostles and prophets, Christ Jesus Himself being the corner stone, in whom the whole building, being fitted together" (Eph. 2:20–21). The progression from the Old Testament tabernacle to the New

Testament church also includes the individualization of God's presence within each believer. Each believer is a part of the church at large, and as individuals assemble, they become the sanctuary of God.

The sanctuary must be unleashed

Earlier, I wrote that when Solomon dedicated the temple, God showed up in such a powerful way that the entire building was filled with smoke. This represented the overwhelming presence of God. When the Hebrews marched through the wilderness and set up camp, the tabernacle was put up first, and the Ark of the Covenant was placed inside a curtained room. The glow of the presence of God was visible from the outside. Now, along these lines, quickly switch to some New Testament imagery: "That He would grant you, according to the riches of His glory, to be strengthened with power through His Spirit in the inner man" (Eph. 3:16).

The power of the sanctuary originates as God strengthens us with his power *from the inside out*. God dwells inside each of us where our "inner man" lives.

The inner man is the real you, the place where

> ❝Heaven's plan has always included an unleashing—the takeover of the earth by the church. ❞

your true motivations originate. The inner man orders the outer man; the outer man simply carries out the wishes and desires of the inner man. The strengths and weaknesses observable in the outer man are simply a reflection of the strength or weakness in control of the person who occupies the seat of the inner man.

This is what the Scripture means when it says God dwells in our inner person, strengthening us with power from the inside out. We are the tabernacle of God, and his presence in our lives should be so evident that the people around us take notice. They should see a difference in our actions and attitudes, but they should also see a difference in our authenticity of life. That is, the way we view life differs from the way they view life. We have a future and a hope; the only future they have is what they create for themselves. The only hope they have is that something or someone won't come along and take it all away.

We certainly need to understand the uniqueness of our identity and know how to utilize our role as citizens of the kingdom. Both our role and power are bound together in our identity as citizen sanctuaries of God.

Yet we've bought into the idea that the evil powers of this world are simply too great for us to defeat. We continue our resistance in hopes of simply slowing down the advance of evil. We think that if we can just hold on until Jesus comes, then everything will be alright. We view our casualties as acceptable for the magnitude of the battle we fight. Yet we have no real hope of any victory until we hear the trumpet of God. We carry on with our church programs, and the occasional social invasion, until the resistance we meet promises losses that we are unwilling to accept. We then back off and regroup perhaps to fight again another day.

This is not heaven's plan for the church. Heaven's plan has always included an unleashing—the takeover of the earth by the church. This is why Jesus came, and it is why he died. His death secured the authority for the takeover, and his indwelling presence provides all the power to ensure completion. The power of God resides within every believer, but, for the most part, it remains a captive resident.

Only as we identify our weaknesses can we correct them. We have chosen to believe the lies of the enemy rather than the truth of our God. We must reverse our course and begin to confess what God knows is already true. We are the sanctuary of God, the dwelling place of his presence, power, and authority.

One of my friends does design work for churches. His job is to create brochures and publicity materials that help a church reach its community with attractive information about services and ministries. The work he turns out is always top quality and very effective.

He told me the other day, though, that he was feeling a bit dishonest about some of the work he was doing. "I know some of the things churches are having me put into their printed material are not as accurate as they need to be. They want pictures and graphics that depict changed lives and power-filled ministries. I produce them, but I know that some of these churches are publishing things the way they *want* their church to be, not how they really *are*."

> **"What people really want is a church filled with the power of God. Give them that, and you can cut the advertising budget in half."**

It doesn't matter how good the printed materials are; if the power isn't unleashed in the sanctuary of God, the people who attend will know it. When power pulses through the sanctuary, people are engaged in the ongoing process of knowing Christ. Without the power of God, high-end brochures and flawless music produce something quite sad: people who come for the show but walk away unchanged. My friend said it best, "What people really want is a church filled with the power of God. Give them that, and you can cut the advertising budget in half."

When we identify our lives with Christ, we also identify our lives with his local body, the church. God has promised that his presence will dwell in his people. Yes, we are individually the temple of God, but we will never fully experience the inner-man power of the presence of God until we are integrated into a local church. Only in the body can we encourage each other and stimulate one another to love and to the expansion of the kingdom of God. So …

Let us hold fast the confession of our hope without wavering, for He who promised is faithful; and let us consider how to stimulate one another to love and good

*deeds, not forsaking our own assembling together, as is
the habit of some, but encouraging one another; and all
the more as you see the day drawing near.*

—Hebrews 10:23–25

I realize that your past experiences with church will prob-
ably affect how you apply this chapter to your life. You may
figure this material sounds good, but you're not sure whether
you're willing to give any church another try. I'm not asking
you to give the church another try; I'm asking you to take the
lessons from this chapter and find a church that lives up to
its calling as the sanctuary of God.

It's obvious that we don't need another church here in
America. On my way to speak this morning, I passed numer-
ous church buildings. Churches everywhere have half-full
parking lots and fully dead ministries.

However, somewhere in your area is a church striving to
live up to the New Testament directives for the living sanctuary. Don't stop looking for it until you find it. When you
do find it, plant your life there. Get involved in the
unleashed power of God and become a part of something
much larger than you could ever be on your own.

Chapter Five

HOW DO I GET PAST THE HYPOCRISY?

Physical fitness is a national craze and a multi-billion dollar industry. Every time you turn on late-night TV, you'll find at least one fitness guru selling his or her latest machine, a contraption that promises to give you the perfect body in return for "just minutes a day!"

Something about these programs being on late-night TV doesn't seem right. The only people who catch these infomercials are insomniacs who seem to enjoy watching several very fit people work out ... while they sit there polishing off a half-gallon of chunky-chocolate-butter-crumb ice cream.

Here's just a sampling of the fitness machines available for six, ten, or twelve easy payments. First, there's the classic Stairmaster and the treadmill with automatic speed and incline control. The reason I like the treadmill the best is because of the full-length support bars that run along both sides of the machine. They're great for hanging drip-dry laundry. Then there's the BowFlex, with all those rods sticking up. The great thing about the BowFlex is that you can put different socks and caps on each of the power rods, put the whole set in motion, and watch your own private Mardi Gras.

The other night, I saw the Gazelle infomercial. Does anyone else besides me have a problem with the fact that a gazelle is an animal that spends over half its life running to avoid being somebody's dinner?

The latest fitness device I've seen is the Pole Runner. It's a sixty-inch weighted metal bar with rubber tips on the ends. The free video instructions show the user how to place one end of the Pole Runner in a stationary position on the floor and then run around in a circle to the beat of the music. Why would anyone pay $29.95 for something like this when he could just as easily go to his cleaning closet and cut the handle off a broom?

Over the past twelve years that I've been on the road, I've tried just about every diet known to man. I've made most of them work, but now I have three sizes of clothes in my closet—large, extra large, and *Oh no! It's coming toward me!* Still, people are always giving me suggestions on how to lose weight. One person said I should take up running because it's really good for me. The only time I'm going to run is when I'm being chased. Somebody else told me to try walking. I tried it several times, but I must have looked wrong doing it. Why? Because every time I walked, several people would stop by at different times to ask where I broke down and if I needed a ride to the nearest service station.

Finally, somebody told me I should join a nationwide gym, so I could work out anywhere I go. These health clubs charge outrageous prices and then have the nerve to offer free weights. Anyway, once inside the gym I tried several of the exercise machines. The thing that's so hard about lifting weights is that they're so ... weighty.

One of the machines in particular annoyed me the most. I followed the poster on the wall that showed how to use it and laid down, placing my feet in what looked like gynecologist's stirrups. I felt like I was about to give birth. (I don't know what the body-builder name for this machine is, but I call it the Gas Master.)

> 66 **The thing that's so hard about lifting weights is that they're so ... weighty.** 99

Just before I gave up on the gym, I finally found one machine that was a natural for me. I had no trouble lifting it or making it go back and forth. I did it for about five minutes with each hand. When I was finished, I walked over to the instruction jock on duty and said, "That one over there is my favorite machine in the room. What do you call it?" He looked where I pointed, squinted, and gave me a scowl. "Vacuum cleaner," was all he said.

Next to the locker room was a large, open room with a wood floor and thirty turquoise and black step decks. People were milling around the room, so I decided I'd go to the back of the room where I could check everything out without slowing the class down for a beginner. The music started, and the leader began barking out drill-sergeant instructions. "Left foot up, right foot up. Right foot down, left foot down!"

Up, down, left, right—I was thoroughly confused. All the while, she kept telling everyone, "Don't forget to breathe!" Now, I've forgotten a lot of things in my life. I've forgotten where I parked, where I put my keys, and the punch line of a joke or two, but I've never forgotten to breathe! The fact that she

> I've been in churches that are run like democracies. In this system, the will of God is established by majority vote.

continually reminded us made me wonder if it was worth it to stick with the class. I mean, would I need to call her several times a day just to remember to breathe?

I really did poorly in this class. My right was her left, and my up was her down. Just when I thought I was the worst student in the class, I noticed a guy all the way down at the other end of my row. He was so bad that he made me look good. I was beginning to feel better about myself when I realized that I was looking in a mirror.

Anyway ... here's the point of all this exercise talk: We all seem pretty obsessed with making our bodies look as good as they possibly can. God is also concerned about *his* body, the church. The challenge is to get that body in shape too. We've got to find a healthy church body to plug into and bring our own spiritual body into shape.

The church sits on the foundation of the message of Christ—how he has changed our lives and how he can change the lives of others. God is building a church full of men and women who are so committed to his purposes that the things God wants to do in the world become noticeable in their lives. This is the gospel "lived out" for the world to see.

As we've seen, the message isn't only about our individual salvation; there's a corporate aspect, too. Since the Bible speaks of the church as the body of Christ, let's dig deeper into what that really means. In Ephesians, the apostle Paul tells us all about what the body is and how it functions. So, as we get in shape, let's put aside our M&Ms and explore the body's Ms: its makeup, movement, maintenance, and mandate.

Find the makeup of the body

[The Father] put all things in subjection under
[Christ's] feet, and gave Him as head over all things to
the church.

—Ephesians 1:22

This verse hints at the structure, or makeup, of the body of Christ. The body has two parts. Christ is the head of the body; we are the members of the body. The pastor is not the head and neither is the church leadership. The person who gives the most money isn't the head, either. Simply put, none of the members of the church are the head of the church. We are not in the business of building our own little kingdoms; we are in the business of building God's kingdom. We are to follow the crown fully, because we are subjects of the crown.

I've been in churches that are run like democracies. In this system, the will of God is established by majority vote. It's a bunch of people sitting around a table saying, "What do you think we should do about this situation?" They take a vote on it and equate their decision with the will of God.

In reality, the church and the kingdom are not a democracy but a theocracy (ruled by a benevolent, divine King). This means churches are ruled by One, not by a majority. In the church as well as the kingdom, there is a crown, and underneath that crown are the citizens. Jesus wears the crown, and we are citizens of his kingdom. But what are these citizens like?

We're individuals, but not private There's no such thing as private Christianity. The individual members of the body of Christ make a mosaic, in which every "piece" has its place. Christ and the church go together. To live without the church is to live without Christ. Being Christian and belonging to the church are inseparable. To be a member of the body means we fully depend upon the head.

One of the most amazing facts about the church is that in spite of how many problems it has had throughout the centuries and how many individual grievances people have with the church, it is still the most successful institution the world has ever known. It is the largest global organism:

There are more churches and believers around the globe than any other institution.

> **"We have to abandon the idea that everyone in the church is better and more holy than everyone else."**

In spite of how crazy the church may look and how disappointing it may have been, it is still the body of Christ made up by one crown, Jesus. The beauty of the church is that God takes his mosaic of people and forms it into one cohesive group. This is why Paul says there is neither Greek nor Jew nor male nor female. Our social status or our skin color no longer identifies us; we are now the body of Christ.

We're natural, then supernatural Now, let's get one thing straight right up front: Never assume that the people of the body are morally superior to nonmembers. We have to abandon the idea that everyone in the church is better and more holy than everyone else. After all, what is the one requirement for admission? *You have to be a sinner.*

The righteous, of course, don't qualify for salvation. So, the church teems with people who are screw-ups, because Jesus "came not to call the righteous." But these people of the body, who are saved because of their badness (not their goodness), are learning to let the indwelling Spirit transform them into something beautiful and holy. It's a supernatural, ongoing process that takes a lifetime—until they see Jesus: "He who began a good work in you will perfect it until the day of Christ Jesus" (Phil. 1:6).

But let's go deeper here. Realize that *before* this supernatural transformation begins in people who open their hearts to Jesus—that is, before salvation—they are in a natural state. *And there are people sitting in church pews each Sunday that are in this natural state as well.*

As we move out of Ephesians 1 into Ephesians 2, we see this before-and-after picture quite clearly as Paul describes the *condition* of the members of Christ's body: "Before" they were natural; "after" they are supernatural. Look in Ephesians 2:1–12, and see what Paul has to say about dealing with the body's condition.

• *We were spiritually dead.* "You were dead in your trespasses and sins" (Eph. 2:1). The natural state of the citizen is that we're born dead spiritually, and we're unattached to God. That is what verses 1–5 are talking about. We come into this world with dead spirits. This means that we have not been brought to life. We have not fully joined ourselves to the life of God.

When the Bible speaks of us being separated from God and people going to hell—as much as we hate to hear stuff

> **66 When you look at the history of the world, it is not about humans being good to one another; it's about humans being selfish. 99**

like that—the reason why they are sent to hell is not because of what they do. Rather, it's because they remained spiritually dead, right into eternity. There was never a moment in which they attached themselves to the presence of the living God.

• *We were followers of the Enemy.* "You formerly walked according to the course of this world, according to the prince of the power of the air" (Eph. 2:2). So, in our natural state, we are dead and followers of the evil one. We are born into this natural order. We are by our very nature destructive and rebellious.

• *We were children of wrath.* "Among them we too all formerly lived in the lusts of our flesh, indulging the desires of the flesh and of the mind, and were by nature children of wrath, even as the rest" (Eph. 2:3). You don't have to go very far to prove that, by nature, we are children of wrath. All you have to do is look at babies. Little kids are selfish, and everything revolves around them. That's the premise of all the movies about kids. *Monsters Inc.* revolves around a kid who cries and freaks all the monsters out. We are all by nature prone to be selfish and self-driven. As a result, we make a lot of bad decisions by which we hurt ourselves and other people.

When you look at the history of the world, it is not about humans being good to one another; it's about humans being selfish. All the wars, strife, and conflict arise out of our own bent toward selfishness. In our natural state, we are spiritually dead and follow the evil one. By nature, we have appetites of destruction.

• *We were separated from God.* "Remember that you were at that time separate from Christ" (Eph. 2:12). Good people don't come to church, but natural people do. In fact, many of you reading this book have gone to churches filled with natural people—unregenerate, unreclaimed people—and you just assume that since they are at church, then they must be believers.

Not so! This is why you can find people in church who do despicable things. I went to speak at a church where, just the week before, a young single couple decided that love couldn't wait ... and neither could their plans for a family. They took their desires to the guy's SUV and, just as the windows were fully fogged, a staff member interrupted them.

People walk into the church and assume that everybody there loves God, but churches are filled with people in their natural state. The Bible is fiercely honest about the type of people in the church. The wheat and the tares grow together until Christ returns (see Matt. 13:24–30). So, everything found *outside* the church exists *inside* the church. There is prejudice, immorality, self-importance, a cutthroat success-at-all-costs mentality, abuse of power, and lust for position and prestige ... there, that takes care of the church staff.

They are in the right place, where they can connect to the life of God and one day, hopefully, they will be brought to life. Or, they may *already* have Christ within them, but he is being pushed aside and sin seems to reign in them, at least for now. It's complicated, isn't it? We see a person doing bad things in a church, but we can't assume a thing about that person's salvation. You see, some folks are believers who have stopped growing and maturing, and they're caught up in sin. Others are indeed unbelievers who are trying like crazy to live good lives, hoping to earn points with God. So they appear so much more moral than the believer who's messing up big-time.

My point is, we just automatically assume when we walk into a church that everybody "gets it" spiritually when they may not. The condition of the citizens is that we all begin in a natural state. We come into this world separated from God. In other words, we are all, by nature, bent on doing destructive things. We are all, by nature, twisted. In order to become part of the kingdom, we have to be reclaimed; we have to know Christ.

> "The Bible is fiercely honest about the type of people in the church. The wheat and the tares grow together until Christ returns."

One of the expressions Jesus uses to talk about reclaiming people is "born again." When you think about it, your first birth gave you physical life. You came into this world screaming and crying and drawing breath. The second birth gives you spiritual life. In order for us to get it and be the body of Christ, something inside of us has to be kick-started. Our spirits have to be brought to life, which is what verse 5 is talking about: "Even when we were dead in our transgressions, [He] made us alive together with Christ" (Eph. 2:5).

Let's consider three things about this supernatural state of soul aliveness. First, something real happens inside of us and brings us alive. Everyone starts out in a natural state. There is a moment where their lives collided with the life of Jesus, and they were brought into a supernatural state. You are either alive or dead. There are not different levels of dead. You are not sort of dead or kind of dead (just as you can't be a "little bit" pregnant, right?). You are either dead or you are not. Until we draw in the breath of the Spirit, we're all dead. Jesus is the life. God brings us to life. The church is the only bona fide institution that is proclaiming this anywhere on the globe. In the supernatural state we are made alive; we have drawn the breath of Christ.

Second, in the supernatural state, we are brought close to God: "[He] raised us up with Him, and seated us with Him in the heavenly places in Christ Jesus" (Eph. 2:6). Our status has changed. The Bible says that we were once far off, but now we are brought near. Some people have been brought up to believe that no matter how much they experience of God, they are always going to be dirt. It sounds very pious or spiritual, but there is no truth in it. Instead, the power of the supernatural life is that we are brought close to God, made near to him.

Third, we become heirs with Christ: "[He] raised us up with Him, and seated us with Him in the heavenly places in

Christ Jesus, so that in the ages to come He might show the surpassing riches of His grace in kindness toward us in Christ Jesus" (Eph. 2:6–7). Everything that is real about Jesus is made real in us. We get to participate with all that he is. We are fellow citizens in the body of Christ. Accepting Christ means that we have been brought alive. We are no longer what we used to be. The breath of God is eternal and has wakened us from the dead.

Now, we must let that supernatural life in us show through in how we act. And as I've said, our actions may be good or bad at any given moment. But we're on an upward trail, growing in Christ, maturing in behavior. If we take a step back sometimes, we may look just like a person who never had Christ's life inside at all. But don't be fooled. Christ will finish his work of perfecting you until the end of your days.

That is the makeup of the body. We start in a natural state. Then, once our life collides with the life of Christ's, we are brought into the supernatural state.

Follow the movement of the body

Now God has placed the members, each one of them,
in the body, just as He desired.

—1 Corinthians 12:18

A body is supposed to have movement. It gives the body perspective in its surroundings and lets it interact with its environment. Consider:

The body is assembled During the first three centuries of Christianity, believers had no buildings they called church. They met in homes and places of business. Their meeting places moved around as necessary to provide the space they needed. It wasn't until the Middle Ages that the parish ministries we now know as churches came into being. Ask the Christians of the first three centuries where they went to church, and they wouldn't know what you were talking about. They were the community of faith, and they gathered in different stores in the marketplace.

They understood that each person in their church had been given an assignment by God. They understood that their individual assignment was coordinated by God to complement every other individual's assignment. The supernatural orchestration of these individual assignments made the maximum impact for the kingdom of God on their town.

The body is assigned Our physical body isn't duct-taped together; rather, each part smoothly transitions to the next part, and all the parts work as a cohesive unit to accomplish the task at hand. The body of Christ is the same. Each part of Christ's body has its own assignment that has been organized by God to work perfectly and in harmony with every other part. In this way, the body accomplishes his plan for the earth.

Whether we know it or not, every believer has an assignment from God. The Scripture calls these assignments "spiritual gifts," and you can find lists of these God-given assignments in Romans 12:6–8 and 1 Corinthians 12:8–11. The gifts are special empowerments from God that members of the body use to build one another up. The assignments listed in the verses above are:

- Prophecy—to be able to discern and speak truth into specific situations. This is not intended as a license for anyone to be sarcastic or mean-spirited. It is to be utilized with care and motivated by redemption.
- Service—cooperating with other believers to accomplish the many tasks required for the ongoing function of the church.
- Exhortation—urging and advising believers to continue living in the way that allows God's presence and purpose to be experienced and seen in their lives.
- Giving—modeling through their own behavior faithful and sacrificial giving in a way that focuses attention on the achievement of God's purposes and motivates other believers to take part.
- Leadership—observable activity by a believer that is seen by other believers as worthy of their own involvement. The leader is chosen by God; the leader does not choose him or herself.
- Mercy—decisive action by a believer that delivers God's compassion to others in their times of need.

Members of the body discover and exercise all these gifts *in the church*. The church provides the context for their functioning; in fact, these assignments don't work outside the context of the church. Your church is the place where you assemble with other believers to utilize your assignments and accomplish the purposes of God for this world. Within the church, you will discover and mature your personal assignment.

Fine-tune the maintenance of the body

Be devoted to one another in brotherly love; give preference to one another.

—Romans 12:10

> " Every time something went wrong, they cut off a member. Such churches don't help the injured; they amputate them! "

The body doesn't stay healthy simply by taking care of the healthy, but by taking care of the *un*healthy. The Scripture says that we are to give preference to each other and make certain that what we need we provide. If one suffers, we all suffer.

A lot of people have been burned in church because they got involved in a body that wasn't taking care of its own. Every time something went wrong, they cut off a member. Such churches don't help the injured; they amputate them! They work like the Tony Soprano family does—"taking care of" their dirty laundry (but the church uses very creative ammunition). On the other hand, a healthy church maintains its health by going to the area of greatest need and nurturing it.

Specifically, how do the members of the body stay healthy? Here are several ways:

We commit ourselves to each other This is authentic community action. We understand that each member is an integral and inseparable part of the whole body. Absent one of us, and we are incomplete. We welcome the attachment we share, and we attend to each other's needs. In fact, we give preference to the needs of others before taking care of our own needs!

We recognize each other's assignments—and encourage their use Several people may have similar assignments, but no two assignments are exactly the same. One may be assigned to serve, as are many others. But not everyone can serve in the nursery (and not everyone could *enjoy* serving in the nursery). Another may be assigned to teach, as are many others. But not everyone can teach middle-school students. The body maintains health as it recognizes and values the assignments of each member.

We love and we walk in unison We neither walk in front of or behind each other. Instead, we share equal responsibilities in the body. Arm in arm, cooperating and complementing the assignments of others, we share a companionship of calling that fosters an ever-growing sense of unity.

We do not allow division in the body Too many churches have been started out of resolvable conflicts. A group of hurt and angry people left the church and began their own congregation across town. But these days, fewer churches are begun because of arguments; people just click off and stay away from the church altogether. In any event, when we face conflict, we'll experience genuine unity when we take all possible steps to resolve it, regardless of the personalities involved or the assignments they carry out.

A common misconception is that a healthy church is made up of healthy people. This is just not true. Instead, a healthy church has members who are experiencing the realities of one another. The members are vulnerable and transparent with one another in their small groups, so that both the healthy and the unhealthy parts come to the surface for prayer. They report the good that God is doing in them, and they also confess their sins. They share their strengths and victories, their weaknesses and failures. What a healthy church! Of course, some body parts have been around a long time; others have more recently been added. Some have idiosyncrasies that we have to learn to appreciate.

We do allow diversity in the body Maintaining diversity in the church is similar to maintaining diversity in a real-life family. There's always been diversity in the ordinary family. You have the tyrannical, dogmatic father who has to have everything his way—do your homework by 7 PM, keep your room clean, and don't interrupt my three hours of TV every evening. He always sets the tone for an agreeable, cooperative evening.

He's married to the activist mother who's actually married to the PTA, and who has taught all of her children how to fix their own sack lunches and how to heat up scrumptious frozen dinners.

> **"A healthy church has members who are experiencing the realities of one another."**

And which of us doesn't know the eldest child who has long ago decided that the best way to keep both mom and dad happy is to live the life of a double agent: one life at home and another they'll never find out about? Then there's the youngest child, who discovered every parental loophole by the time he was three.

Rounding out the extended family is the uncle who can't seem to make his own way in the world. He's lived with the family for several weeks, following every one of his six divorces. And finally, there's Grandma in the nursing home. She doesn't remember anybody, but everyone still tries to visit her regularly (that is, at least until she dies and her will is settled). The point of all of this is that in the midst of all the diversity, *this is still a family.* Unity does not necessarily mean conformity. A healthy church has honest members who are encountering the presence of God in healthy ways.

In this mosaic, you'll find people in the church who are on their way to becoming believers and people who are already believers in Christ. There are people who have been broken by life, and there are people who know addiction from both sides. A healthy church is *not* made up of entirely healthy people; it is made up of people in various stages of health who regularly experience the presence of God in community with other believers. They are all sinning to some extent while walking this pathway toward holiness.

As the body of Christ grows in relative health, it meets new experiences that will demand more than the body has ever given before. The body cannot stay the same and meet the demands placed before it. There is a clear mandate for the body of Christ.

> 66 We need to leave our childishness, when we used to believe that we had to feel everything for it to be real. 99

Fulfill the mandate of the body

> *Speaking the truth in love, we are to grow up in all aspects into Him who is the head, even Christ, from whom the whole body, being fitted and held together by what every joint supplies, according to the proper working of each individual part, causes the growth of the body for the building up of itself in love.*
>
> —Ephesians 4:15–16

The mandate of the body is simple: *Grow up!* Keep maturing in spiritual growth. We have to ask ourselves, though, *how* do I grow up? Some of us have been trying to grow up on our own without any help, away from the body. We've been operating as spiritual free agents, and if there is any spiritual progress in us, it's minimal.

One of the reasons is our attachment to subjectivity. We need to get rid of all the speculation: "I always heard ... I was always told." No, we need to leave our childishness, when we used to believe that we had to feel everything for it to be real. Then we won't be tossed around by every crazy idea that comes down the pike.

Another sign of spiritual maturity is that we speak the truth in love. We no longer have to rip into everybody who disagrees with us. I meet a lot of people who know a lot about God, but they are hateful about it. How childish! These people actually know too much, and they are dangerous with what they know until their actions catch up with their intellects.

Most importantly, maturing Christians are coming to realize that individual success is ultimately determined by their corporate identity. All of us *together* need to get the body in shape! We've got to live out all that God created us to live and to be. Mature. On the most practical level, we do it by letting him grow the fruit of the Spirit in our lives.

The fruit of the Spirit is love, joy, peace, patience,
kindness, goodness, faithfulness, gentleness, self-control.
—Galatians 5:22–23

These are the believers' marks of maturity in the faith.

When these character traits shine through in the lives of believers, we know they're growing. Paul first spoke of the marks of maturity to a community of faith in the territory of Galatia. The aspects of the fruit of the Spirit are personal, in that they are observable through our lives. But their true meaning only becomes apparent as we interact with other believers in the community of the church. Here's what these character traits might look like in action:

Love—drawing attention to the true nature of Christ when displayed in other believers and, at the same time, not drawing attention to their faults.

Joy—experiencing gratification in the experiences believers share while living out the purposes of God.

Peace—together, finding harmonious solutions to conflicts in the church.

Patience—refusing to let frustration have its way in the body of Christ.

Kindness—exercising compassion and releasing forgiveness before it is sought by anyone else in the body.

Goodness—choosing to be gracious and generous when we have every reason not to be.

Faithfulness—willingly keeping promises and commitments, regardless of the consequences.

Gentleness—not demanding our own way or advancing pure self-interest.

Self-control—not letting our instincts take us to a place that would break the heart of God.

The mandate of the body is maturity, or growing up in Christ. If we want to see this kind of fruit in our lives, we must be a part of the body of Christ.

There will always be hypocrisy in the church. But we cannot accept hypocrisy as an excuse to keep us from being a part of it. Instead, we must see the hypocrisy as *the reason* for our continuing to be a part of the church. Perhaps we can even serve as change agents, leading those around us into greater stages of maturity.

Chapter Six

WHERE HAS ALL THE POWER GONE?

The church has its own unusual atmosphere. If you've attended church at least once, you know that it's different from just about any other place on earth. Where else can you sit for an hour on uncomfortable wooden benches while trying to sing karaoke accompanied by a pipe organ playing melodies you've never heard ... and then be forced to shake hands with twelve smiling strangers who normally wouldn't give you the time of day in a Golden Corral buffet line?

Follow that delightful experience with a thirty-minute lecture on a topic of which you know absolutely nothing. It's delivered by a speaker who either puts you to sleep with his monotone delivery or sends your mind on a quick search for the nearest mental foxhole. How else could you shield your fragile psyche from the barrage of haranguing religious legalisms? And then ... they pass the plate.

But not before the soloist mounting the platform picks up the microphone and says, "Y'all please pray for me while I sing this song." (This is church code for, "I haven't had any time to practice this week, and I'm not sure how this is going to sound.") She gives the nod to the sound guy in the back of the room, who presses the Play button on a cassette machine. After ten seconds of silence, the music begins. The singer listens to a few bars for her cue and then waves to the sound guy: "Earl, that's the wrong side of the tape." She then tries to "share a few words of testimony" (church code for stalling) while everyone waits for Earl to rewind the tape.

With experiences like these as our primary impressions of church, is it any wonder that people would choose to replace it with just about anything? Many people I talk with wonder why anyone willingly chooses to get out of bed for such craziness.

Nevertheless, the church is Christ's idea. He birthed it in the first century following his crucifixion, and its early development comes to us in the Book of Acts. As Jesus ascended to heaven, he told his disciples to return to Jerusalem and wait until the power of heaven came upon them. They did just as Jesus had told them and waited in the Upper Room for days.

They did not wait in vain. The power of God arrived on their lives. It showed up as small flames above each of their heads. (If you think I'm kidding, read Acts 2:1–3). The noise emanating from the room must have been quite loud, because lots of people came to check out what was going on. The waiting disciples went outside where a crowd had gathered, and Peter delivered his first sermon (see Acts 2:14–36). His message was short but powerful, and over three thousand people became Christians that day. This was the beginning of the church. The remainder of the Book of Acts chronicles the actions of the church as it spread throughout the first-century world.

One of the early church's greatest challenges was dealing with the city of Rome. By the fourth century, the church had Christianized most of its inhabitants. Talk about power and influence! From three thousand converts on that first day four centuries earlier in Jerusalem to nearly every inhabitant of Rome, the church permeated every part of society—even the money. Previously, Roman coins had displayed images of pagan gods; now, because of the influence of the church, those images were removed. And during this same period, the church heavily influenced public policy. Politicians enacted laws that benefited the continued growth of the church throughout the Roman Empire.

How was it that a small group of disciples could start something so small but, in just four centuries, it would transform a city the size of Rome? How is it that they could do something so great without special music, skits, mimes, pancake breakfasts, puppets, or bingo? How was it possible to do what they did without large sound systems, big-screen video projections, and tour buses? What was it about them that made even

> **"What did these guys have? What did they know that enabled them to turn city after city upside down?"**

their enemies say: "These [people] *that have turned the world upside down* are come hither also" (see Acts 17:6 KJV).

What did these guys have? What did they know that enabled them to turn city after city upside down? The Book of Acts shows us that these men were propelled by four beliefs and/or approaches that enabled them to change the culture of a city. These beliefs and methods are not as mystical as you might think. In fact, they are already possessions of everyone who has come into Christ, but they are, for the most part, simply unutilized. Every effective church operating as a redemptive community already possesses what the disciples had:

They were convinced of the Messiah's uniqueness

Peter stood up and preached the sermon we read in Acts 2. This is the same man who three times denied that he even knew Jesus on the night of crucifixion. Listen to what Peter says: "Therefore let all the house of Israel know for certain that God has made Him both Lord and Christ—this Jesus whom you crucified" (Acts 2:36).

Peter is saying, "You people killed Jesus!" As a speaker, calling your audience a bunch of murderers isn't the best way to win friends and influence people. Just a few weeks before this, the entire city of Jerusalem was shouting, "Hosanna! Hosanna!" to a man humbly riding into town on a donkey. That same man, only days later, would again capture the attention of the city when he was tried in both the public and religious courts for his claim to be the Messiah. Following the trials, he was led through the streets in an ironic reenactment of his entrance into Jerusalem. Only this time, the crowds shouted something quite different: "Crucify him! Crucify him!"

Peter referred to Jesus as *Lord* and *Christ*. The word *Lord* tells us that Jesus is "the one in control." The word *Christ* means, "The anointed one (who can carry our burdens)." Peter was saying to the people of Jerusalem that the Jesus they crucified was uniquely the Son of God; there was no other like him, at that time or forever. Jesus was not "one of the more powerful sons of God," as if there were other sons of God. He was saying that Jesus was the only one, whom God had sent to be the *Lord* of all and the *Christ* of all.

The cities of the day were filled with multiple influences; Greek, Roman, and Jewish traditions all had a part in the society of the day. In many cities, idol worship was not only acceptable but a required part of life. All sorts of dark influences operated with free rein. But then and now, Jesus *still is* the only one of his kind, God's unique Son. He is able to carry away the sins, the stains, the scars, the static, and the screwups of every person on the earth. At the same time, he *is* the only one who is able to control life. He is both Lord and Christ of the earth.

The early disciples were convinced of all these things about Jesus. Are you? Is your church? "Who do you believe Jesus to be?" The answer to this foundational question makes up the underpinnings for all of Christianity, in all times and places.

The turning point of the battles we face in our personal lives revolves around our individual convictions about the uniqueness of Jesus the Messiah. Either we are able to handle our own mistakes and failures—in which case, we become our own Messiah—or we already recognize the fallacy in this thinking and trust the unique position Jesus holds as our Messiah.

What changed the lives of the people in Jerusalem changed lives in Rome four centuries later. It wasn't the music, cool sermon content, multimedia presentations, or dramas. It was the life of Christ made authentic in the lives of people convinced that he was the Messiah.

They were compelled by a universal mission

Peter's words describe the wide-ranging mission of the church: "The promise is for you and your children and for all who are far off" (Acts 2:39). Thousands gathered that day in Jerusalem, but Peter already knew that the mission of the church would extend far beyond those city walls.

On the day he left them to return to heaven (Acts 1:4–8), Jesus told his followers that they would receive power to be his witnesses and that their mission would begin in Jerusalem and continue throughout the entire earth. These men remembered Jesus' words and understood that what had taken place that day held worldwide implications. They looked beyond Jerusalem into the countryside surrounding the city. They looked beyond that into the entire country of Israel. They looked beyond their own country's borders and saw the entire world exposed to the Messiah's influence. This is the mind-set they brought to the mission.

I believe Jesus is coming back, but he may not be coming back in our lifetime. That is, not if we don't get to work. Many of us have been trained to sit and wait for the world to come to an end. We wait for it to blow up and glibly throw out such phrases as, "Bless God; it's getting darker." We've got Christians applauding the outbreak of AIDS; they see it as a sign of the end times. Can there be any more anti-Christ emotion than that—to cheer for the advance of evil just so we can escape the world? This certainly wasn't the mind-set of the first-century church. They saw the entire world in need of the Messiah, and they were convinced only he could make the difference the world needed.

Their world had just as much evil in it as ours does today. They didn't sit in their Upper Room hoarding the truth and all the power of God for themselves. They stepped outside and proclaimed the truth for everyone to hear. Then they set about the task of taking that message to the world beyond their doorstep. Happy or sad, married or single, gay or straight, rich or poor, whoever wants to come can come. The scope of their ministry must become ours: "Let anyone in."

They carried with them an upsetting message

The crowd gathered outside the disciples' Upper Room heard Peter's words and were "pierced to the heart." They called out, "What shall we do?" And Peter told them, "Repent, and each of you be baptized in the name of Jesus Christ for the forgiveness of your sins; and you will receive the gift of the Holy Spirit" (Acts 2:38).

Their message was revolutionary and fresh. It flew in the face of everyday expectations in a world filled with messages of segregation—"Every group besides ours is wrong, and you're not welcome in our group." The message of the believers, though, was inclusion—"Anyone can come, and we don't expect you to be perfect; you aren't expected to be good enough or moral enough. You simply have to want to come."

Their world was filled with cliques just like ours is today. Judaism had its subgroups—Pharisees, Sadducees, and the zealots—each group thinking it had the corner on truth. The rest of the world was pagan, and every group was led by a different god. Representations of gods, carved and molded into idols of all shapes and sizes, appeared everywhere. Then there were the politicians and the elitists. In their world, everything was exclusive, and only certain people could enter the privileged ranks.

> **I still find churches compelled by a homogeneous mind-set that limits their acceptance only to people of a certain color, politics, dress, or behavior.**

But these believers stood up in the power of God and said, "Whoever wants the promise can have it!" In their mind, there were no boundaries to Jesus, not race or ethnicity, not politics or economic status. There was nothing to keep anyone from coming to Jesus.

It is unfortunate but true. I have seen firsthand the

opposition such a vision of ministry can receive. I still find churches compelled by a homogeneous mind-set that limits their acceptance only to people of a certain color, politics, dress, or behavior. Their church signs may say, "Everyone Welcome," but anyone falling short of that group's minimal expectations will soon face silent stares, closed body postures, and perhaps outright snubs.

I have known pastors of some of these churches who, when they challenged this inbred way of thinking, were asked to leave and find another church to preach in. Because they shared an early church type of worldwide vision for ministry, some have even lost their lives.

But look closely at the first-century message: "Repent, and each of you be baptized in the name of Jesus Christ" (Acts 2:38). Their message is clear. Everyone is invited, and anyone can come. There is only one stipulation: Anyone who comes must come through Jesus. It requires acknowledging personal sin and repenting. This message is upsetting because it is both inclusive and exclusive.

Of course, I realize that churches struggle to define the fine line between the all-inclusive call to new life and setting legitimate boundaries of behavior or lifestyle among the membership. Some churches are so tolerant that they resemble a community center. They have lost their ability to take a firm stand on any subject for fear of offending someone with their message. Other congregations are exclusive to the point of turning away people who express a genuine interest in knowing Christ. These seekers may be unwilling to change their lives upfront in order to measure up to a church's subjective standards. Can we still welcome them to keep on seeking? Surely we must not establish any criterion other than Jesus to become part of the church.

The early believers understood that their message was much more than an invitation to join a new clique or subculture. They knew their message would challenge the way the world thinks and would upset people with its radical grace and love. But they shared it anyway. The message they took to the world was that anyone could get into God's kingdom, and it didn't matter about their past life. God was calling sinners, and everyone qualified. Jesus' blood paid the price for all (see Eph. 2:13).

Somehow we've taken this powerful message of redemption and "dumbed it down" in hopes of making it more acceptable to everyone. Someone once gave me a premoistened towel—you know, the kind that comes sealed in the little foil packet? The outside of the package had a message with the heading, "How to Wash Away Your Sins." One church I spoke in had scheduled a revival and was handing out prepackaged Rice Crispy bars with the name "Revival Bar" printed on the package.

Do you think the church would have changed Rome if it had done similar things? What if they had set up a booth in front of the Coliseum and handed out plastic stick-on fish? Even if they had stuck one on every chariot in the parking lot, do you really think it would have had the same impact as their raw-boned message of God's broken heart for them?

Somehow I don't think they sent the young people down to the corner for a chariot-wash fundraiser in hopes that their presence in the community would "raise awareness" about Jesus.

> 66 What if they had set up a booth in front of the Coliseum and handed out plastic stick-on fish? 99

The church didn't change the world by passing out tracts or wearing cheesy, preprinted slogans on their togas. They changed the world by the message of Christ crucified. Yes, it upset the norms of the day, proclaiming Jesus as both Christ and Lord. But they just couldn't keep it a secret subculture. They openly shared it with their lips and their lives. They were out on the streets every day, playing for keeps.

We carry the same message: "Whoever wants to come can come! Anyone can get into the presence of God, but he must come through Christ. Whoever comes through him becomes a true child of Abraham, becomes a part of the true Israel, the church." They changed the world because they let that message out. But their message wasn't the only thing the world found upsetting and odd. Their approach was quite unusual, too.

They changed the world with unusual methods

[They] kept on exhorting them, saying, "Be saved from this perverse generation!"

—Acts 2:40

> **"Which is the right way to be baptized? Do you get hosed down, sprinkled, or do you have to run through a Water Wiggle?"**

The early believers weren't trying to make their message more acceptable by imitating the surrounding culture. They remained true to their identity and drew society to *their* culture.

Before I identify and define the tools the early church used to change the world, I want to make it clear that every church member has the same tools available for use today. Regardless of the denomination you support, the powerful tools used by the first-century church are available for our use.

Everywhere the early church was established, believers used these six tools to accomplish the kingdom mission. No matter what else happened in their city or town, the influence of the mission remained the same.

Teaching *"They were continually devoting themselves to the apostles' teaching"* (Acts 2:42). The teachers of the church would stand and teach new believers about their new life in Christ. Find five minutes to read through Peter's sermon in Acts 2:14–36, and you'll see that he actually quotes five passages from three books in the Old Testament: Psalms, Joel, and 2 Samuel. The early church teachers didn't have the complete Bible as we do today. They had the Old Testament, and they used it as the foundation of their teaching to prove the uniqueness of the Messiah and to validate the church's position as the new Israel. Teaching from the Old Testament was essential if new believers were to understand and adopt the new covenant mind-set.

Baptism *"Those who had received his word were baptized"* (Acts 2:41). In our world, we've made baptism a battlefield. Which is the right way to be baptized? Do you get hosed down, sprinkled, or do you have to run through a Water Wiggle? Do you get shot with a water gun? For some people, it's a small "sprinkle sprinkle," and for others, it is a full-on slam dunk. The battle over baptism has kept many people away from truly discovering the message of Jesus.

The Greek word *baptidzo* (translated in the Bible as "baptize") means "to immerse"; but that's not the point. For the early church, baptism was a tool. It wasn't just an ordinance tacked on to the end of the service or a nice ceremony serving as a child's right of passage.

When the early church baptized anyone, something crucial was happening. Yes, the church accepted anyone and offered its teaching to all who wished to receive it. Through this teaching, people would understand their need for Jesus and trust him as their Christ and Lord. They were undergoing a soul-deep transformation. Baptism was more than a symbol of this; it was the church's tool for publicly marking an individual with the new life Jesus gives.

The new believer would stand in the water in full public

view. A church leader would stand with that person and say something like this: "Until now, you have been completely immersed in your old way of living. Your old motivations and values buried you there." Then he put the convert under the water. The leader would then say: "Jesus has come into your life and raised you up out of the grave of your old life." As the convert's body rose back to the surface of the water, he or she would hear the words: "You have been raised to walk in a brand-new life."

When baptized people stepped back up on the bank of the river, they understood that their lives were forever different and that they could never truly return to their old way of living. The early church used baptism as a tool to change the world. It became the concluding step in the rebirthing process because it forever identified the individual with Jesus.

Communion *"The breaking of bread"* (Acts 2:42). Sharing communion helped the believer remember that Christ's death was not only a past event but also a permanent reality. With regular communion, believers wouldn't lose sight of the One who was the source of their faith. Reaffirming this reality sealed their allegiance and brought all the members of the community into unity as the body of Christ.

As they took communion, the believers were renewing their commitment to Jesus and one another, reminding themselves of who they had taken into their lives. There was power in this service of worship. Communion wasn't something they did on a Sunday night once a quarter, or a ceremony they held once a year at midnight Christmas Eve. It was a tool for whenever they met together.

Many people trusted Jesus to be their Christ and Lord and were taught and baptized. Then they would sit and receive communion with the other believers. The union and brotherhood for accomplishing the mission was constantly being strengthened.

Discipline *"Everyone kept feeling a sense of awe"* (Acts 2:43). This is a topic hardly ever mentioned in today's church. We've assumed that if somebody ticks you off at church, you just don't go back.

Not so in the early church! When the actions of a member blocked the flow of ministry, the leaders would exercise discipline. Sometimes the offender was put outside of the community due to unwillingness to change and make things right. Such discipline kept the mission moving forward throughout the city.

Today's church has twisted the purpose of discipline. Now it is used to push people out of the church if they get a divorce or if they're just too different from the rest of the people. But when the early church saw selfishness, arrogance, and immorality, they confronted it. They knew that, if left unchecked, such actions would damage the church's witness and mission. They were committed to having an environment where God could dwell in power.

Scriptures and creeds *"Day by day continuing with one mind in the temple"* (Acts 2:46). The early church used worship to teach the truths of Scripture. Often leaders would lead the people in singing Scripture or reciting hymns and creeds aloud together. This would reinforce their common beliefs as they learned theology while singing.

The church members were taught how to use the Word of God accurately so they could back up their beliefs with Scripture. I meet a lot of people who don't have a clue about Scripture. They quote Ben Franklin and give credit to the Bible: "God helps those who help themselves." The Scripture is one of the church's greatest tools for ensuring mission success. Like the early Christians, we must take advantage of our opportunities to study it and learn how to handle it accurately.

Pastoral ministry *"Many wonders and signs were taking place through the apostles"* (Acts 2:43). The early church leaders treated their position as a tool to build the kingdom of God. They faithfully delivered the message of Jesus and did signs and wonders like he had done. God enabled these leaders to do signs and wonders. He also empowered their teaching and their preaching. Through these pastoral ministries, the world was turned upside down.

So … are we ready to pour the supernatural into our culture?

I'm aware that it might seem as if I'm opposed to skits, video clips, and object lessons in a church's worship service. The truth is, I'm all in favor of creativity in communicating God's truth. But too often, today's church uses these "tricks of the trade" to try and slip a spiritual "mickey" into the world's gin and tonic swill of life, hoping that, over time, people might develop a taste for all things spiritual. The first-century church approached its mission in just the opposite fashion. The dynamic of the church was the supernatural. They took the undiluted message of Christ and poured it straight-up, freely offering the supernatural water of life to anyone who would drink.

When the supernatural fills the church, we won't need a video clip of Indiana Jones to fill it with seekers. We won't need *Star Wars: Attack of the Clones* to remind us to be true to our identity in Christ. We won't depend on *The Gladiator* to inspire us to stand firm against the schemes of the devil. (And we will no longer need to see *Dumb and Dumber* to know that drinking after other people can be dangerous to our health.)

> **When the supernatural fills the church, we won't need a video clip of Indiana Jones to fill it with seekers.**

The power of the supernatural permeated the first-century church. Here's an example: Rome boasted elegant bathhouses (best described as houses of bisexual ill repute). These buildings were huge, ornate with colorful decorations. Out front, large pillars decorated the entrances. Inside, multicolored glass in the ceilings filtered the light flowing into the rooms. Marble floors and plush draperies made it all quite luxurious.

As more and more people came to know Jesus, though, the myriad bathhouses lost their business. Before long, most were taken over as church worship centers! About that same time, the new emperor of Rome, Constantine, replaced the Roman eagle with a cross and had it painted on all the soldiers' shields.

Now, flash-forward to our day. Our churches are built to include stained-glass windows and pillars in the front—and many have marble floors. These architectural trimmings came from the bisexual bathhouses of Rome. They are current-day testimony of the church's ancient invasion of Rome.

So, what would happen if every Hooters became a house of worship? What would happen if the local bars had to shut down for lack of business? What would happen if people came and touched the very presence of God through our worship? They would hear the Word boldly taught and empowered by God. They would receive ministry, and signs and wonders would take place. Our churches would grow as they have not grown since the fourth century.

Could you get out of bed for something like that?

We have the same beliefs as those leaders of the early church. We have either never realized what we are holding, or we have never learned how to release its power.

We've seen that the role of the church is to bring to life the kingdom of God in our cities. Our prayer has to be: "God, help me understand my role in the community of faith, and show me how to support what you're doing in this city." Society is by no means beyond hope. It can be changed, but only when supernatural power flows in the same way it was bursting out in the first century. Are you ready to be a part of that? If so, get deeply involved in your community of faith. Work hard to bring the message of grace and hope to a hurting world, until the day ...

When Christ, who is your life, appears,
then you also will appear with him in glory.
—Colossians 3:4 (NIV)

READERS' GUIDE

*For Personal Reflection
or Group Discussion*

Introduction to the Readers' Guide

The Questions for Life series gets to the heart of what we believe. Sometimes our church experience hardly seems worth the effort. *Did I Get Out of Bed for This?* is a question many Christians ask at some point. As you read through this book, use the discussion points in the following pages to take you to another level. You can study these points on your own or invite a friend or a group of friends to work through the book with you.

Whether you are just checking God out or desiring to go deeper in your relationship with him, let yourself be challenged to change the way you live based on the answers you discover to life's most pressing questions.

Chapter 1: Who would God marry?

1. In what areas of your life have you sacrificed the most? How does this feel to you?

2. What is the ongoing mission of Jesus, and how do we partner with it?

3. How do we help spread the kingdom ethic around the globe? How would this look in your own neighborhood?

4. What role do you play in the service of the bride? How do you know?

5. To what extent do you think the church as a whole has been faithful in birthing the purposes of God into the world? Name some examples of success or failure.

6. What are the weapons of the church? How do you, personally, use each of them?

Chapter 2: What's the deal with church people?

1. Why do you think some people view God as a self-imposing lawyer figure? What is your own God image? Why?

2. Do you think your church lives out a new covenant mentality? How do you know?

3. What is the makeup of your church's mosaic? What kinds of people make up the total picture?

4. What power has the church been given, and how are we to use it?

5. What are some ways that the power of the community can be seen? When was the last time you saw it most clearly?

6. How would others in your group describe the kind of "church person" you are?

Chapter 3: Did I get out of bed for this?

1. What happens if the individual parts of the city don't work together?

2. What frustrations challenge your new identity? Be practical!

3. God paid a high price for the church. Do you think what we do in church is worthy of that price? Explain.

4. What has been compromised in the church when we focus solely on the number of attendees? What other focuses would you like to see? What could be your own role in such changes?

5. In your observation, where is your church most impacting its surrounding culture? Where does it need to have more impact? How could it take a first step?

Chapter 4: Why can't I TiVo church?

1. What inherent value does every church have? In what ways have we forgotten this?

2. What address change did God make in the Bible?

3. What difference does it make if we see ourselves as *citizens* of the church rather than mere *members*?

4. Describe the responsibilities we have as the temple of God. What does this mean for the way you live your daily life? Can you share a specific example?

5. What would happen if the power of God was unleashed in your church? What would that look like?

Chapter 5: How do I get past the hypocrisy?

1. What is the only hope for those who are in a natural state? How would you describe your spiritual state these days?

2. What happens when our natural state collides with the life of Christ? What has that looked like in your own life?

3. In what ways are you fulfilling the assignment God has given you?

4. What does it mean to be a healthy church? Name some key characteristics.

5. Based on the marks of maturity, how mature are you? What do the other members of your group think? (Take some time to affirm one another with the good you see!)

Chapter 6: *Where has all the power gone?*

1. What are some of the burdens that you would like to trust Jesus with?

2. How big is our mission in this world? How big is your personal mission at the moment?

3. What about the gospel makes it upsetting to our generation? Where do you see this most powerfully?

4. What is the postmodern reaction to the church's exclusive message? What is the reaction of your own friends and acquaintances?

5. What effect has our watered-down theology had on our ability to impact the world? What solutions would you suggest?

The Word at Work Around the World

A vital part of Cook Communications Ministries is our international outreach, Cook Communications Ministries International (CCMI). Your purchase of this book, and of other books and Christian-growth products from Cook, enables CCMI to provide Bibles and Christian literature to people in more than 150 languages in 65 countries.

Cook Communications Ministries is a not-for-profit, self-supporting organization. Revenues from sales of our books, Bible curricula, and other church and home products not only fund our U.S. ministry, but also fund our CCMI ministry around the world. One hundred percent of donations to CCMI go to our international literature programs.

CCMI reaches out internationally in three ways:

· Our premier International Christian Publishing Institute (ICPI) trains leaders from nationally led publishing houses around the world.

· We provide literature for pastors, evangelists, and Christian workers in their national language.

· We reach people at risk—refugees, AIDS victims, street children, and famine victims—with God's Word.

Word Power, God's Power

Faith Kidz, RiverOak, Honor, Life Journey, Victor, NexGen — every time you purchase a book produced by Cook Communications Ministries, you not only meet a vital personal need in your life or in the life of someone you love, but you're also a part of ministering to José in Colombia, Humberto in Chile, Gousa in India, or Lidiane in Brazil. You help make it possible for a pastor in China, a child in Peru, or a mother in West Africa to enjoy a life-changing book. And because you helped, children and adults around the world are learning God's Word and walking in his ways.

Thank you for your partnership in helping to disciple the world. May God bless you with the power of his Word in your life.

For more information about our international ministries, visit www.ccmi.org.

Additional copies of *Did I Get Out of Bed for This?*
and other NexGen titles are available
from your local bookseller.
Look for the other books in the Questions for Life series:

Why Is it Taking Me so Long to Be Better?
What Happens When I Die?
How Safe Am I?
Has God Given Up on Me?
Why Is This Happening to Me?

If you have enjoyed this book,
or if it has had an impact on your life,
we would like to hear from you.

Please contact us at:

NEXGEN BOOKS
Cook Communications Ministries, Dept. 201
4050 Lee Vance View
Colorado Springs, CO 80918
Or visit our Web site: www.cookministries.com

NE✗GEN®

Building the New Generation *of Believers*